ISOLATED

ISOLATED

TWO PLAYS

Greg MacArthur

Coach House Books

first edition

 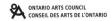

Published with the assistance of the Canada Council for the Arts
and the Ontario Arts Council. We also acknowledge the Government
of Ontario through the Ontario Book Publishing Tax Credit Program
and the Government of Canada through the Book Publishing
Industry Development Program.

LIBRARY AND ARCHIVES CANADA CATALOGUING IN PUBLICATION

MacArthur, Greg, 1970-
        Isolated : two plays / Greg MacArthur.

Contents: Get away – Recovery.
ISBN 978-1-55245-191-5

        I. Title. II. Title: Recovery. III. Title: Get away.

PS8625.A78I86 2007   C812'.6   C2007-905245-2

CONTENTS

INTRODUCTION

A note on how to boil a frog alive:

If you drop a frog into a boiling pot of water, he will flail about, scream, jump out of the pot and hop to safety. However, if you drop a frog into a lukewarm, seemingly refreshing pot of water, he will loll about. Make funny little froggy fart bubbles. Pound some old Beach Boys tunes against the steel walls of the pot with his feet. You know, kick back and relax.

Then, turn up the heat. Slowly. Incrementally. Bit by bit. The frog will stay put. Maybe he'll start to feel a bit uncomfortable. A bit feverish, a bit dizzy and sweaty. 'I'm coming down with something,' he'll think to himself. 'Whatever. It'll pass. Relax. Take a nap. I'll feel better in the morning.'

Then, turn up the heat some more The water starts to bubble slightly. The frog becomes a bit disoriented. The steam is making his eyes water. His balance is off. He thinks to himself, 'Something's up, something's different, something's not right.' He notices some sores on his legs. An irritating cough that won't go away. 'Anyway. It's probably nothing. A shift in the weather. Something I ate. Don't be paranoid. Everything's fine. Anyway, the bubbles are kinda fun. Like a water park. Ride it out. Everything's fine.'

Then, turn up the heat some more. The water starts to boil vigorously, violently. Scorching hot. Steam fills the pot. The frog is delirious now, panting, throwing up: he's lost four toes, the skin is peeling off his face. There's a piercing scream in his head. He tries to find a way out. He's lost. He's weak. He calls for help. It's too late. He has no voice. His eyes melt. His brain fries. His body splits open. Everything falls apart.

❖

Both these plays are inspired by horror movies. I enjoy horror movies. I enjoy being scared. I enjoy putting myself in the victim's situation. I enjoy wondering how I would behave in their shoes. If I became possessed by the spirit of a rabid dog, if a dead Japanese child crawled out of my mouth, if a pack of zombies were chasing me through the woods, what would I do? Would I crumble and panic? Would I rise to the occasion? Would I pick up the axe, head off into the woods yelling 'Fuck you, zombie bitch!' Or would I say 'Please, please don't. This would kill my mother. I still have a lot to accomplish in my life. My friend is right over there behind the sofa. Take him instead.'

Both these plays explore what happens when normal everyday folk find themselves in extreme situations. This is the essence of horror. There are no villains. There are no heroes. We can all be extraordinary. We can all be despicable. We are all full of surprises.

Mostly, life doesn't happen in bursts, in grand epiphanies or strokes of enlightenment. Mostly, life happens slowly, incrementally, in small ways. It creeps up on you. Like a zombie. Or love. Or fascism. Until it's too late to do anything about it.

The question will inevitably come up: who are these characters speaking to? The obvious answer is: the audience. Keep in mind, this can include many possibilities: friends, policemen, politicians, documentary filmmakers, teenagers, murderers, lovers, next-door neighbours, barflies, the deaf, the blind, the bored, the disenchanted, the hopeful. There are many ways to approach these plays. Be bold, be adventurous, be dangerous.

– Greg MacArthur
Montreal, July 2007

GET AWAY

Get Away premiered at Alberta Theatre Projects' Enbridge playRites Festival of New Canadian Plays in February 2005.

David: Patrick Galligan
Henry: Jesse Dwyre
Garbo: Adrienne Smook

Director: Glenda Stirling
Lighting design: David Fraser
Set design: Scott Reid
Costume design: Jennifer Darbellay
Sound design: Jonathan Lewis
Stage manager: Cheryl Millikin
Dramaturge: Vanessa Porteous

It was subsequently produced at the Westbury Theatre in Edmonton, Alberta, and at the Old Red Lion Theatre in London, England.

The creation and development of this script was supported by the Toronto Arts Council, the Canada Council for the Arts, Playwrights' Workshop Montreal and the 2004 Banff playRites Colony.

For Sionnach and Saiorse.

CHARACTERS

DAVID *(late thirties)*

HENRY *(a teenager)*

GARBO *(a teenager)*

PART ONE

SCENE ONE

DAVID: (*to audience*) Oh, you know, these things happen incrementally.

One night, I put on a piece of music I've always enjoyed listening to. What do those record magazines call it? A desert island disc.

And the music, which used to wrap itself around me and lift me up, well this time it just sat there. Limply. All over the carpet. Kind of twitching around me, but not touching me.

I took it off the CD player and put it back in its case. I walked outside and buried it in a park across the street.

I went back inside and locked the door.

I sat in a chair, very still.

Not long after, I started feeling it all around me. In my food. In my bed. In the newspaper. In the faces of children.

My friend had a funny name for it. What did she call it – ?

Henry and Garbo appear, with bowls of cereal.

HENRY: Mm, this is –

DAVID: Do you like the cereal?

HENRY: It's really delicious. It's satisfying.

DAVID: I used to enjoy eating cereal at night, like a snack before bed.

HENRY: It's ... what is it?

DAVID: Honeycomb.

HENRY: Honeycomb. Is that – Is that the one with the bear on the carton?

DAVID: It comes in a red box. I don't remember a bear.

HENRY: The Honeycomb bear. Isn't there a – ?

DAVID: I don't remember a bear.

HENRY: Am I making this up?

DAVID: Perhaps you're thinking of Sugar Crisp.

Pause.

HENRY: Well. Anyway. It's damn good. (*to Garbo*) Isn't it?

GARBO: It really hits the spot.

HENRY: Fancy cereals don't come our way too often.

DAVID: You looked like you could use something … a boost … so …

GARBO: (*to Henry*) A boost?

HENRY: (*to Garbo*) He read us like a book. (*to David*) You read us like a book.

DAVID: I just thought, you know –

HENRY: 'There's a couple of wacks. A couple of hooligans. Ruffians.'

DAVID: No, I thought –

HENRY: 'A couple of nogoodniks.'

Pause.

DAVID: You've got a unique vocabulary for someone your age.

HENRY: I pick things up. Here and there.

GARBO: He's got a mind like a steel trap. Is that what they say?

DAVID: I thought you could use a hand, that's all. A leg up.

HENRY: It's generous of you. To take us in.

DAVID: A good night's sleep.

GARBO: You got a heart of gold. We can see that.

DAVID: Oh, I don't know …

HENRY: It's neighbourly. Sitting here with us. It's adventurous.

DAVID: I wasn't doing anything, so, I mean, why not –

HENRY: We could be a couple of psychopaths.

DAVID: I'm not uncomfortable around young people. I mean, people younger than me. Some people are.

HENRY: Not you.

DAVID: No.

GARBO: Yeah, you've been pretty chill with us.

Pause.

HENRY: Of course it's a risk for us as well. A stranger. Inviting you in for a bowl of cereal.

Garbo looks at Henry.

(*to Garbo*) Could be a snatcher. A molester. A child pornographer. What do you think?

GARBO: He don't strike me as a child pornographer.

DAVID: Oh, well, I'm not so –

Pause.

I do confess to owning a copy of *The Blue Lagoon* once.

Henry and Garbo look at him blankly.

A movie. Brooke Shields and Christopher Atkins. A kind of … um …

HENRY: I remember liking a movie called *Ghost*. I remember getting all sad over that one. It was on TV. You remember that movie?

DAVID: Yes. Demi Moore. She was involved in pottery.

Pause.

DAVID: If you want some more cereal –

HENRY: I'm stuffed like a pig.

GARBO: I feel all jumpy. In my stomach.

HENRY: Maybe a sugar high.

DAVID: I guess it's not the healthiest late-night snack, but –

Pause.

HENRY: It's nice in here. It's cozy.

DAVID: There's a lot of wood. The walls, the furniture. I think it gives it a kind of –

HENRY: This table is something.

DAVID: It's not mine. It came with the place. With the rental.

HENRY: It's sturdy. I can see a little family sitting around this table. A Pilgrim family, maybe.

DAVID: It's an antique. Probably. I don't know. I'm guessing.

HENRY: What makes an antique? Would a Pilgrim's table be considered an antique?

DAVID: I'm not really an antiques dealer or anything –

GARBO: Or a child pornographer. We're really starting to narrow the field.

Pause.

DAVID: There's plenty of room. You can sleep on the rug by the fire. I can bring you some quilts.

HENRY: Maybe right here on this sturdy table.

DAVID: There's plenty of room, so –

HENRY: Is there anything we can do for you? You know … some painting? Yard work? Small home repairs?

DAVID: They have a department for that at the rental agency. If there's a problem you just call them and they send someone over, I imagine.

GARBO: A hotline.

DAVID: You pay for it. For the service. For the convenience. It's all part of the package.

HENRY: Well, how 'bout I clean up?

DAVID: You don't have to.

Henry disappears with the cereal bowls.

You have really nice skin. A really healthy complexion.

Pause.

I used to know people who'd spend a fortune on creams and ointments to get a complexion like that.

Pause.

I knew a woman who actually injected something into her face.

Pause.

Not herself. At a clinic. Even still –

Henry appears.

HENRY: I'm just letting them drip-dry, if that's okay.

DAVID: That's fine. Thank you.

Pause.

DAVID: I was just telling your – I was telling Garbo what a beautiful complexion she has.

HENRY: What do they say? Country air.

DAVID: Yes.

HENRY: And clean living.

DAVID: I could use a bit of that, I suppose.

HENRY: What?

DAVID: What?

HENRY: Country air or clean living?

DAVID: Oh, both, I imagine.

GARBO: You got a nice head of hair.

David smiles.

DAVID: How about I get you those quilts?

David disappears.
Henry looks at Garbo.

HENRY: You've got some cereal or milk or something on your mouth.

Henry touches Garbo's face.
David appears with two folded cotton quilts.

HENRY: Wow. Now those are a couple of nice items. Those are a couple of items worth taking care of.

DAVID: They came with the place. You can wrap yourself up in them, sit on the porch and ... watch nature, I suppose.

GARBO: They go nice with the wood.

DAVID: Well, if you need anything –

David hands them the quilt.

GARBO: Good night.

Henry and Garbo disappear.

SCENE TWO

DAVID: *(to audience)* At first they thought it was viral. The word 'airborne" was mentioned. Someone told me they thought it had something to do with one's diet.

And then there were those who just refused to believe anything was happening at all. You know, burying their heads in the sand and all that. But for me at least, it was impossible to ignore.

Things started to be left unattended. Bicycles. Dog shit. Cellphones. Children.

Everyone became a bit blurry-eyed.

I watched a teenager walk directly into a brick wall. He just sat there on the pavement, a little trickle of blood dripping off his forehead onto his K-Way jacket.

One night, there was a report on the radio that a group of people was going to be setting off some fireworks in a park downtown. They handed out sparklers to some of the younger children. But instead of running around in circles making patterns of sparks in the night, the children all just kind of stood around randomly, watching them fizzle out.

There was a bit of a movement. A resistance, if you could call it that. Some people banded together.

They would gather in public spaces across the city and try to instigate random conversations with strangers. And singalongs.

Well, you couldn't blame them. No one really knew what to do. We were all kind of wandering around like scared little puppies, so –

Sometimes I would call up my friend to talk, you know, to commiserate. Misery loves company. All of that. We'd go for coffee, or sometimes for a drink. I'd sit down across from her and just start blabbering on about, I don't know, me.

Well, eventually that became unbearable.

I couldn't listen to myself talk anymore. The same words coming out of my mouth. I would get halfway through a sentence and I would just stop, out of sheer boredom.

Words like 'discontent', 'exhaustion', 'perplexed', 'isolation'. They didn't mean anything. They didn't hold any more weight than, say, I don't know, hat, or pen, or silo, or dirt. This friend of mine actually suggested I start keeping a diary. Jesus Christ, I thought to myself. I have far too much respect for pen and paper.

I actually did write a few lines one night in my bedroom, in an old address book that had some blank pages at the back for scribbling notes.

I don't exactly know why I had an address book. I never wrote letters and rarely visited anyone, so –

So, I remember writing a few lines about, I don't know, my state or the state of the world, and I drew a little picture of a … a penis … or something … with a face and some of those dialogue bubbles you see in comic books.

God, I thought, a three-year-old could be more creative.

I remember telling someone – we were talking about tattoos (this was ages ago) – and I said something like, 'I wouldn't know what to get. Nothing sticks with me. I am a creature of fads. A faddist.'

A loud sound.
Henry appears naked. He is wrapped in the quilt.

HENRY: I'm sorry.

DAVID: Is everything all right?

HENRY: Did I wake you up? I woke you up.

DAVID: I thought I heard something.

HENRY: I banged my foot. That table –

DAVID: The leg kind of sticks out. I should have left a light on.

HENRY: I shouldn't be creeping around in the dark.

DAVID: Do you need anything? Are you warm enough?

HENRY: A glass of water. It's a bit dry in here.

DAVID: The wood really absorbs the moisture. I was thinking about getting a humidifier.

HENRY: Do you mean a vaporizer?

DAVID: Well, no. I think they're similar, but –

HENRY: Because I think you might have some trouble finding a vaporizer around these parts.

DAVID: That's true.

HENRY: Or a humidifier, for that matter.

DAVID: It's the fireplace. It sucks up all the moisture.

HENRY: You could put a pot of water by the fireplace.

DAVID: That's true.

HENRY: Or some plants. That might help.

DAVID: Maybe.

Pause.

HENRY: Jeepers creepers. Listen to me, keeping you up, talking about humidifiers. It's, what, three in the morning? I'm sorry. I'll just –

DAVID: It's all right. I'm a light sleeper.

Henry disappears.

SCENE THREE

DAVID: (*to audience*) The epidemic started to accelerate and spread. I started to hear rumblings from various corners of the world.

The inhabitants of an entire island in the Caribbean – this is what I heard – all gathered on a beach one bright morning and walked into the ocean.

There was a rumour an entire village in the South African countryside just stopped breathing one day.

Insects and bees started just hanging around in the sky. They seemed to have no desire to pollinate or sting anything.

Flowers lost their odour. Herbs lost their flavour. Everything seemed to taste the same. Like dried noodles.

Apparently there was a good Indian buffet across town that still managed to serve up a decent meal. The owner was a small man who kept his spices in a sealed container in his fruit cellar. The papadums were always crisp, and there was a good spicy yogurt dip, I was told.

And so one afternoon – I hadn't eaten in about three days – I thought I would take myself out to lunch.

When I got there I had a sudden wave of lethargy.

There was a long table full of cutlery and dishes of food. A few people lined up. The idea of having to serve myself – getting in line with a tray and tongs, getting my own silverware – it all seemed like too much effort.

I stood outside. I didn't know what to do. I mean, should I stand there, should I walk somewhere else, should I lie down on the pavement?

Looking around, I noticed an advertisement taped to a telephone pole. 'A remote getaway. A cabin in the woods. Peace of mind.'

There was a picture of a raccoon or a chipmunk or something. And a phone number.

And so the next morning, I put some of my clothes into a suitcase.

I left the city.

It seemed that somewhere, deep down, there was still a seed of hope. Somewhere, a desire to save myself.

Henry appears, holding one of the quilts, which is rolled up and covered in vomit.

HENRY: I'm so sorry.

DAVID: It's fine.

HENRY: A lot of work went into this. A lot of handicraft –

DAVID: I'm sure it's replaceable.

HENRY: You'll probably have to pay for it. The rental agency is probably gonna slap you with a bill.

DAVID: It's fine.

HENRY: Did you put a deposit down on this place? Do you have contents insurance?

DAVID: Look, I'm sure it's all covered in the agreement. It's –

HENRY: I take full responsibility.

DAVID: It's no one's fault.

HENRY: Garbo's always had a sensitive stomach. We've been eating a lot of tuna fish lately. Some cheap brown grapes. An old avocado we found in the parking lot. I think the cereal was too much for her. The sugar content.

DAVID: I'm sorry. I didn't know –

HENRY: Why would you? You're not a dietitian. Are you?

DAVID: No.

David takes the soiled quilt and examines it.

DAVID: I think this will clean up. The smell is worse than the stain. I think a good soak –

HENRY: You bring us into your nice rental cottage. You offer us a leg up. And what do we do? We interrupt your nice rental vacation. We puke all over your nice rental quilt.

DAVID: Look, there's a label here. It's from a department store, so – It's not a big deal. It's cheap. An imitation.

HENRY: Department store goods don't always come cheap.

DAVID: Where is she? Is she – ?

HENRY: I put her outside. Fresh air.

DAVID: Shouldn't you go check on her?

HENRY: People are embarrassed after they puke. They like to be left alone.

DAVID: Well, I'll just go soak this in some water.

David disappears with the quilt.
Garbo appears with the box of Honeycomb cereal. She grabs a handful and starts to eat.

HENRY: He seems tidy and polite. There's plenty of space. A fireplace and a big bathtub. A hammock and a barbecue. What do you think?

GARBO: This cereal isn't very good on its own. It really needs some milk or fruit or something.

SCENE FOUR

David appears.

DAVID: Oh, you're –

GARBO: The hair of the dog. Is that what they say?

HENRY: That's what they say.

Pause.

DAVID: Well – I soaked it in some hot water. I hung it out. Good as new.

HENRY: R-e-l-i-e-f. What does that spell?

GARBO: That spells relief.

DAVID: I wasn't really worried.

HENRY: You're a real renegade. Some people would get all worked up. Some people would go ballistic over something like this.

DAVID: It's not mine, so –

HENRY: Fuck it. It's only puke. Like they didn't puke on quilts in antique times. I bet it happened all the time.

GARBO: Eating caribou and shit. Eating wild berries and mushrooms and beaver and shit. I bet it happened all the time.

DAVID: You're probably right.

HENRY: Even still, it's good of you not to freak.

DAVID: It's just a quilt.

HENRY: A rental quilt.

DAVID: Yes, so –

HENRY: So we're square. You take us in. Give us a leg up. I do your dishes. Garbo pukes on your quilt. I feel bad. You wash it up. Good as new. We're square.

DAVID: Yes. I mean, it's been fine. It's been –

GARBO: You weren't doing anything.

DAVID: No.

HENRY: A real heart of gold.

DAVID: I wasn't doing anything, so …

Pause.

HENRY: Are we keeping you from something?

DAVID: No, I'm just –

HENRY: If you've got something –

DAVID: No.

HENRY: We can leave.

DAVID: I've got nothing –

HENRY: (*to Garbo*) What do you think?

GARBO: Let's go.

DAVID: You don't have to – Please. I mean –
If you want to stay for a few days – If you want to stay with me – For a few days –

Henry and Garbo disappear.

SCENE FIVE

DAVID: (*to audience*) It was very remote. In that respect, the advertisement was accurate. As for the rest, peace of mind – I mean, did I feel any different?

I don't know.

I would go outside and sit on the porch, and ten minutes later I would be back inside staring at the walls.

I would lie in bed at night and listen to myself breathe.

Sometimes, out of sheer boredom, I would drive into town to browse through the grocery store aisles. I bought things I don't eat and don't like.

I don't like Honeycombs.

I tried making conversation with the grocery store clerk. She looked at me strangely. Kind of disgusted and terrified. All I said was something like, 'Your produce is much cheaper out here than where I come from.'

Every day dragged on. I felt like I was aging years at a time.

I didn't find any comfort in solitude or trees or the sound of birds.

I sat in my cabin alone and thought, 'What the hell am I doing?'

The thought of going back to the city, though –

And so I ended up just kind of wandering around, on the road, in the woods, in town.

Music, in the distance.

That's when I started seeing them.

Camped out on the road at the edge of the forest, huddled under a plastic sheet. A kind of makeshift tent.

Two kids. Well, teenagers.

I'd see them in town behind the dumpster. Or on the sidewalk by the grocery store.

Sometimes they would play with each other's hair, or throw small rocks at a pop can.

Sometimes they would be rooting through bags of garbage.

Sometimes they would be singing. Or dancing. Side by side.

Funny little steps.

One night they were both asleep on the grass under the grocery store sign. I walked over to them and stood there, looking at them. They were using their shoes for a pillow. I crouched down beside them. I sat there for a few minutes.

The moon lit up their faces. I watched their eyelids flicker. I just –

I don't know. The two of them. Lying there together. All tangled up.

I felt myself truly inhale for the first time in months.

Someone drove into the parking lot. They slowed down and looked at me suspiciously. I got up and walked back to my car. I drove back to my cabin.

I thought about them, out there lying on the ground. I thought about me, in here climbing walls.

After that, I started keeping an eye on them. Showing up where they were, you know, coincidentally.

Garbo appears, reading an entertainment magazine.

GARBO: Did you read this article?

DAVID: What's that?

GARBO: It's about this new Korean film director.

DAVID: Yes I did, actually.

GARBO: I think I could be in movies. I have good skin and I enjoy people looking at me. What do you think?

DAVID: I knew a group of actors once. They had their own company and they would put on performances in this abandoned shopping mall. They weren't a very successful group of people.

GARBO: I didn't say I wanted my own company, I was just thinking –

DAVID: I went to one of their shows once.

Barely anyone was there, and I spent most of the time picking dead skin off my lips.

GARBO: Oh, and there's this funny story here about this fourteen-year-old actor who was charged with sexually molesting his sixty-seven-year-old makeup artist.

Garbo disappears.

SCENE SIX

DAVID: (*to audience*) One day I was walking into town. I thought I might get myself a deck of cards or a piece of fruit or something.

After walking for about forty minutes, I came across their plastic tent. I crept up and looked inside. The two of them were asleep, curled up together.

I noticed a piece of paper taped to the side of a tree. A little homemade poster. 'Henry and Garbo. Tonight. Midnight. $5. Limited seating.'

Henry and Garbo.

I arrived at the tent a little early. There were a few candles in tuna fish cans under the plastic, lighting it up. Everything else was dark and there was no one around.

There was a basket outside the tent with a sign. '$5 please.'

I stood around for a while, not knowing what to do.

Eventually a woman showed up with a kid, maybe five or six years old. She was smoking. He had a puffy coat on over his pyjamas.

The woman finished her cigarette and threw it in the admission basket.

The kid crawled into the tent. The woman went back to her car.

I took out a five-dollar bill and put it into the basket, on top of the cigarette.

I crawled inside and sat down cross-legged. There wasn't a whole lot of room.

I accidentally bumped the kid in the stomach. He gave me a dirty look.

We sat there for a while and nothing happened.

Suddenly, we saw shadows coming towards us and heard music. The back of the tent opened up and –

Henry and Garbo appear.

HENRY: (*to audience*) We found a bag of clothes in the dumpster beside the grocery store. Garbo got herself a colourful sweater with a big collar and a flower-print dress. I got myself a button-down shirt, a pair of wool socks and a hat with a small feather. At the bottom of the bag, there were a couple of video cassettes, a few utensils, some old photographs, pot holders –

(*to Garbo*) What else?

GARBO: I don't know. A stuffed animal, um, a bottle of perfume, a few old magazines …

HENRY: (*to Garbo*) And … ?

GARBO: (*to audience*) And a song book.

HENRY: (*to audience*) A hit parade of American classics. All your favourites from the twenties, thirties and forties. For organ and voice.

We didn't know any of the songs and we didn't read music. We didn't have an organ. But anyway.

We put on some of the clothes and flipped through the songbook.

GARBO: (*to audience*) They were dead people's clothes. As soon as you put them on, you could tell. They were heavy and, I don't know, limp. I tore the arms off the sweater and made a vest. Henry looked like a million bucks in his new hat.

HENRY: (*to audience*) I read some of the lyrics out loud. Funny old words that made Garbo laugh. I made up little tunes. Garbo hitched up her skirt, danced around a bit and sometimes joined in with the singing.

GARBO: (*to audience*) Henry has a nice high voice.

HENRY: (*to Garbo*) Thank you.
(*to audience*) Garbo ended up having a good ear for harmonies, and she wasn't too shabby with the footwork.

GARBO: (*to audience*) Thank you.

HENRY: (*to audience*) A couple walked by and threw us some money. Things took off from there. I learned some of the songs by heart. Garbo got more complex with the dancing.
Sometimes we drew a crowd of five or six people. Garbo had the notion of putting together some kind of midnight cabaret in the woods.

GARBO: (*to Henry*) We could put candles around the tent and charge admission.

HENRY: (*to Garbo*) That's a good idea.

GARBO: (*to Henry*) Thank you.

HENRY: (*to audience*) Garbo's got good ideas coming out the wazoo. She's always coming up with something.

GARBO: (*to audience*) I picked up one of the photographs we found in the garbage bag. It was this young couple standing side by side. The boy was holding a guitar. The girl had stars in her eyes. On the back someone had written their names: Henry and Garbo.

Henry and Garbo disappear.

DAVID: (*to audience*) I looked over at the kid. We didn't know whether it was appropriate to clap or not. We sat there for a bit, wondering if there was going to be an encore or something. The kid eventually crawled out of the tent and went back to the woman in the car. They drove away.

I didn't want to leave. I sat and watched the candles flicker. I didn't know if I should blow them out or not.

Outside, Henry and Garbo were holding the money basket, looking kind of disappointed.

I told them how much I enjoyed their performance.

We started to smell smoke, something burning. One of the candles was too close to the edge of the tent and was burning a large hole in the plastic. The whole thing started to collapse.

Their tent was ruined and it was cold outside.

I invited them back to my cabin to stay the night.

One night turned into two. Et cetera, et cetera.

I told them they could put their belongings – a couple of small knapsacks – in the closet off the main room.

I bought them each a toothbrush and matching bathrobes. I cooked food for them and washed their clothes in the big sink outside.

I got to know them.

Garbo was quiet and liked to observe things. Henry was more, I don't know, obvious with his affections.

We became more and more comfortable with each other.

In the mornings, I would lie in bed and listen to them walk around the cabin. They tried not to wake me up. Their feet made sounds on the wood. The sounds were like medicine to me.

At night they took long baths and sang songs to each other.

I sat on a chair. I watched hot steam come out from under the bathroom door. I crawled towards it and breathed it in. I lay on the floor next to the bathroom door, in the steam, in the music.

My face red and damp. My nose running, everything awake.

Henry and Garbo appear in matching bathrobes.

GARBO: What are you doing?

DAVID: Oh –

HENRY: Are you all right?

DAVID: Yes. Um –

HENRY: We take too many baths. We're using up all the hot water.

DAVID: No, it's –

HENRY: (*to Garbo*) We shouldn't use up all the hot water.

DAVID: It's just –
It's the steam. The wood, you know, it's starting to warp around the doorframe. From the moisture. So –

HENRY: Maybe a fan or something.

DAVID: Yes. That's a good idea.

HENRY: You could put one in the window. It might be good for the smoke, too. From the fire.

DAVID: God, you're really thinking, aren't you?

GARBO: Henry solves things. It's just the way he is.

Henry and Garbo disappear.

DAVID: (*to audience*) They spent most of their days sleeping in, or working on their music. They would hide themselves away for hours at a time. Sometimes outside, on the porch. Sometimes in the bedroom.
They said they were putting together something new. New songs, a new act. It was going to involve props, instruments and costume pieces.
I got them whatever they needed. Wool socks, a hatchet, a small set of bongo drums for Henry.
They sometimes asked for a bit of cash. Not much. $10 here. $20 there.

I would organize little events and outings for us. Croquet tournaments, Sunday drives, picnics.

I was becoming more and more adventurous in the kitchen. Trying out new recipes, cooking with new sauces, using new appliances. Sometimes the grocery store would have a promotion, you know, 'Buy this new waffle iron and get a free pack of waffle batter, a waffle cookbook and some waffle oven mitts.'

Things like that. A sausage maker. A Crock-Pot.

The meals usually turned out badly.

I'd stick the appliances in the back of the closet, forget about them and make some nachos or something.

Some nights, after dinner, they would perform a little excerpt for me. We'd sit around the fire and they'd sing to me.

Their voices wrapped around me and held onto me.

I felt things start to open up.

Little by little, they took up more and more space, and there was less and less room for anything else.

And so, in a little cabin, in a little forest, happiness started creeping back into my life.

SCENE SEVEN

Henry appears.

HENRY: (*to audience*) David.

We were the sunshine of his life.

The smallest thing – a wink or a nudge or a question – and he would light up. It was easy to make him happy.

I told him we were working on a new song dedicated to him. He started giggling, kind of puffed up and got all … wobbly.

Days piled up. We lost track of time. It was the longest we stayed in one place.

I really enjoyed the hammock. I'd swing back and forth, make up songs, play the bongo drums.

Sometimes, David would crawl into the hammock. I'd sit beside him on the ground. I'd rock him back and forth.

Garbo –

Well. She can be a tough nut to crack.
She has trouble relaxing into things.
I told her to try and make more of an effort.
I didn't want her to spoil everything.

SCENE EIGHT

David and Garbo appear.

DAVID: This has been fun. This past little while. This has been –

HENRY: You've been real generous.

DAVID: I mean, I don't want to get all sentimental, but –

HENRY: You've been a real hostess with the mostest.

DAVID: I get that from my mother. Always arranging things, filling up glasses, giving out napkins, picking things up.

HENRY: Well, that's you.

DAVID: Can I get you anything else? I think we've still got some cannelloni left.

GARBO: No.

DAVID: Or some –

GARBO: No.

DAVID: Remember a few weeks ago when we were outside under the tree and that nut … or … acorn … or … nut … it fell on the table, right into the salsa dish, and Henry, you said, 'Everybody make a wish,' and you fished it out with your hands and started flicking chunks of tomato at us? (*He laughs.*)
    I was just thinking about that. Jesus, there was salsa everywhere. All over the table. All over our clothes.

GARBO: I don't remember that. I don't remember a nut.

DAVID: That was after the sangria. We dragged a blanket outside and had a Mexican picnic. Sangria and nachos. We put up balloons and Henry made a piñata.

GARBO: I remember that, but –

DAVID: You fell asleep and Henry and I carried you inside. We put you in front of the fire and cleaned you up.

GARBO: I don't remember the nut.

HENRY: Garbo doesn't have a taste for sangria. Do you?

GARBO: Apparently not.

DAVID: We were all pretty drunk. Henry taught me the flamenco dance. Remember, Henry?

HENRY: Well, I don't know if it was the flamenco dance, that's really Garbo's department, but –

GARBO: What did you wish for?

DAVID: What?

GARBO: The nut. When it fell in the salsa.

DAVID: Oh –

GARBO: What did you … ?

DAVID: Nothing.

Henry and Garbo disappear.

SCENE NINE

DAVID: (*to audience*) It was getting colder at night. The rug by the fire was starting to aggravate Garbo's back, and the cabin was drafty.

Luckily, my bed was big enough for three.

We would pile onto the mattress, all of us, and get under the blankets. Henry and Garbo would curl up together on one side of the bed and me on the other.

During the night I would manoeuvre myself in between them and kind of force myself into the middle.

In the morning we would all be tangled up together.

I would usually wake up before them, and I would lie there feeling their skin against my skin.

Their sweat on me. Their saliva on me.

Sometimes Henry would wake up with a small erection. He would run to the bathroom to do something about it, I suppose.

Garbo and I would stay in bed and pretend to be asleep.

Sometimes they would ask me questions about my life or the world.

I would be purposely vague, or tell lies. The less they know the better, I thought.

People are mirrors. I didn't want to stain them.

Henry and Garbo appear, holding a large paper bag.

HENRY: What's this?

DAVID: Oh, just a little something.

GARBO: You do too much.

DAVID: It's not much. It's nothing. Just something –

GARBO: It's too much.

DAVID: Go on. Open it.

Henry opens the bag and takes out three identical coon-skin caps.

HENRY: Wow.

DAVID: I picked them up at the grocery store. In that bin with the dishrags, Frisbees and, you know, old cosmetics. I was saving them for a special occasion, but –

Henry distributes the caps and they all put them on.

DAVID: Look at us. The Waltons.

HENRY: Your generosity just keeps going and going. It's starting to get embarrassing.

GARBO: Are these –
(*to Henry*) What are these?

HENRY: Coon-skin caps. Genuine coon-skin caps.

DAVID: Yes. Well, no, I don't think they're genuine, but –
I mean, they're probably just souvenirs. Pretend, you know, like plastic tomahawks or –

HENRY: Well, it sure feels authentic. It's like I got a real animal sitting on my head.

DAVID: A friend of mine used to wear one of these. A long time ago. In the city. In winter. With a long leather coat. She was a real trendsetter. In a few months, they were popping up everywhere. You know, in bars and clubs. Well, I saw them. It reminded me. And I thought, 'What the hell?'
I thought, you know, winter's coming and –

Henry, imitating some kind of small animal, crawls over to David and nibbles at him.

HENRY: Garbo, come show David your appreciation.

Garbo doesn't move.

DAVID: Just a silly hat.

Henry and Garbo disappear.

SCENE TEN

DAVID: (*to audience*) This friend of mine – the one who wore the coon-skin cap – I remember she was really into collage for a while. Everyone had their own way of dealing with the epidemic. My friend had this ridiculous idea she could save herself through arts and crafts.

    She collected stray bits of newspaper. And labels and pieces of light metal.

    'There's always something lying around,' she would say. 'that has a bit of magic in it.'

    I don't know. At that time, the idea of acquiring more things seemed frightening.

    I didn't know what to do with what I had.

    I'd see a book in my apartment. Or a candle holder. Or an old battery. And I'd think, 'What is this doing here? What am I going to do with this? Why do I have this?'

    The whole idea of a collage seemed completely frightening to me. Random things thrown together.

    But it caught on. She created a collage circle. Instead of going out, you know, to a movie or for a coffee, people would congregate at her house and they would spend days together locked away, making things.

    These people would literally become physically excited when they found some unique bit of trash to bring to the circle.

    They would hang their collages all over the city. On lamp-posts, in trees, from bridges.

    Little talismans. Protective charms. Keeping the wolf at bay.

    I went once and glued a piece of Melba toast from a cheese plate onto a piece of cardboard.

She died. My friend.

At the funeral, I kept looking at the smooth surface of the casket and thinking that maybe we should glue some, I don't know, macaroni or something onto it.

As a tribute.

Henry appears, with a birch-bark canoe.

DAVID: What is that? Is that a –

HENRY: It's a canoe.

DAVID: God, it is.

HENRY: With a paddle.

DAVID: Jesus, it's really authentic. Where did you –

HENRY: I found a nice long piece of birch bark out in the woods.

DAVID: In the woods? What were you – ?

HENRY: Down that hill, out back.

DAVID: Well, it's really impressive. You've got a knack.

HENRY: I used some small twigs.

DAVID: I'm not very handy with bark. You'll have to show me how you did this.

HENRY: It's for you. A token of appreciation. I thought you could put it somewhere. Like a centrepiece or something.

DAVID: Well. Wow. This is really –

HENRY: I'll go put it on the night table, beside the bed.

DAVID: Where's Garbo?

HENRY: She's still out there, in the woods.

DAVID: I don't think I like the idea of you two being out there on your own. Things can happen. You don't know –

HENRY: You worry too much.

Henry disappears.

SCENE ELEVEN

Garbo appears, holding a stick.

GARBO: (*to audience*) We saw him watching us. Standing behind trees. Sitting in his car, in the parking lot.
    A loner, we thought. He wore nice clothes and seemed to spend a lot of money at the grocery store.
    What the hell, we thought. Things were getting stale. We were sleeping under a plastic sheet and we were hungry all the time.
    He lived in a cabin with a bathtub, a fireplace and a kitchen. Money didn't seem to be a problem.
    Youth and beauty can take you far in life.
    He invited us to sleep in his bed. During the night, he would kind of pry himself in between us and cover himself up with our arms and legs. Like he was trying to hide from something.
    He didn't try anything inappropriate.
    He wasn't completely unattractive.
    Henry would lie around in the hammock with his bongo drums and write little songs.
    I would roll up the rug in front of the fire and practice my dancing. I was teaching myself the mambo.
    David would sit in a chair watching me, kind of grinning at me, saying things like, 'That looks really professional.' Or, 'I think you're onto something there.'

He bought me a new pair of shoes with a hard rubber sole. The shoes made clicking sounds on the wood. David would clap along when I danced.

It was … uncomfortable.

Henry thought it would be a good idea if we did something for him. A gift, you know, to show our appreciation. He thought maybe something homemade like artwork. Something he could keep around and look at.

Henry made a lame canoe out of a smelly piece of birch bark.

I fell asleep on a patch of moss under a tree.

A branch fell on top of me, which woke me up.

David appears.

DAVID: I was worried about you. You were gone a long time.

GARBO: I fell asleep under a tree.

DAVID: It's probably not the best idea to be falling asleep out there alone.

GARBO: I was with Henry.

DAVID: I just think –

GARBO: Where's Henry?

DAVID: He's outside, on the porch.

GARBO: There's a little stream down that hill. I think I saw some deer or something. Is that possible? Deer? At this time of year?

DAVID: Oh, I don't think so.

GARBO: Well, something. It ran past me.

DAVID: You've got to be careful out there. If anything happened –

GARBO: What would happen?

DAVID: I'm just saying –
Things can happen.

Pause.

GARBO: Where's Henry?

DAVID: He's on the porch, I said. He's lighting the barbecue. We're going to roast some corn I got at the grocery store. You wrap it up in tin foil and just throw it on the flames. The whole husk. It's apparently really tasty.

I don't really like corn if it's off the cob. What is it called – niblets or something? Especially creamed corn. I don't like the texture.

You should get cleaned up. You've got dirt all over yourself.

GARBO: Here's a stick. I thought you might like it.

Garbo gives him the stick and disappears.

SCENE TWELVE

DAVID: (*to audience*) After dinner I was in the kitchen cleaning up. Washing things, putting scraps away. A hunk of butter. Some potato salad. Cobs of corn, half-eaten.

I picked up the ones left on Henry and Garbo's plate. I held onto them. I looked at their teeth marks, which made small patterns on the cob.

'Little hieroglyphics,' I thought. Signs of life.

I wrapped them up in a paper towel and put them in the cupboard for safekeeping.

Henry and Garbo were by the fire working on a new song. I thought I detected a bit of a reggae flavour to it.

I finished clearing the table.

We had some beer, and there was still some left in the

bottom of their glasses. Backwash, you know. It was a dark beer, and they found it too heavy.

I picked up Henry's glass. His hand prints and lip marks all over it.

I was about to toss it, but I stopped.

I drank it.

It was warm and flat. I swished it around in my mouth before I swallowed it.

I could taste him.

I picked up Garbo's glass and shot it back. I could taste her.

I went to bed early while they stayed up and watched the fire. I could still taste them, lingering on my tongue and in my mouth when I went to sleep.

Henry and Garbo appear.

GARBO: Henry. Let's go. Henry?

PART TWO

SCENE ONE

DAVID: (*to audience*) I woke up in the night.

I felt a draft on my feet. I thought maybe a window had been left open, or a door.

I climbed out of bed. I stumbled around in the dark.

They were gone.

I turned on the lights. I looked around the cabin. I looked in the closet.

I went outside. I looked on the porch. I looked in the hammock.

I looked for signs of a break-in. I thought maybe some maniac was wandering around stealing children.

Maybe –

I tried to think it through. I tried to be logical.

I went to bed. They were by the fire. I heard soft reggae rhythms. I drifted off. Then –

I didn't know what to do. I stood in front of the fireplace shivering, picking little balls of lint off my pyjamas.

Henry and Garbo appear.

GARBO: What are you doing?

DAVID: Oh. God. There you are.

GARBO: Are you all right?

DAVID: Yes. I mean, but, I woke up and –

HENRY: We were just outside. Out there. In the forest. Not far.

DAVID: I didn't know –

HENRY: Just a hop, skip and a jump –

GARBO: Just down that hill. Past those trees.

DAVID: It's just –
　　　　It was late and I woke up and you weren't here, so –

HENRY: We're sorry.

GARBO: We couldn't sleep. We thought, you know, some fresh air.
The moon. The trees.

DAVID: Yes.

GARBO: The stars. The sky.

DAVID: No, no, it's nothing, I just thought –

HENRY: We should have told you. We should have left a note.
　　　　(*to Garbo*) We should have left a note.

DAVID: I'm sorry. I'm a bit of a worrier. I get that from my mother,
always –
　　　　Um – Overreacting. I lose an umbrella or a scarf and I –
　　　　I panic.

HENRY: You shouldn't panic. Here we are.

DAVID: I'm sorry.

HENRY: You're shivering. Let's get you into bed.

DAVID: (*to audience*) We crawled into bed. The three of us. We pulled
the blankets overtop of us. I touched their fingers. We fell asleep.

HENRY: Good night.

Henry and Garbo disappear.

SCENE TWO

DAVID: (*to audience*) That kind of thing started happening more and more. Henry and Garbo disappearing into the forest.

At night, after dinner, they would slip out.

They said they were working on their music. They said it was better outside. The night air inspired them. The music echoed off the trees.

I didn't want to stand in the way of creativity.

I told them to bundle up and bought them each a pair of thermal gloves. I bought them a couple of heavy hooded sweaters.

I told them to be careful. I always left a light on.

At night, when they were gone, I would putter around the cabin, distracting myself, waiting for them to come home, thinking up new and exciting activities for us to do together.

Karaoke nights. Fashion shows. Home renovations.

Things started to feel –

Um – Things started to feel –

Garbo appears, wearing small fur wristbands.

GARBO: We're going out.

DAVID: Again? It's late. Where's Henry?

GARBO: Outside. He's waiting for me.

DAVID: Maybe I'll come with you. I'll grab some sleeping bags and we can camp out.

GARBO: We need to be alone. This new song, it's sticking us up a bit, so –

DAVID: Build a fire, look at the stars, tell ghost stories.

GARBO: We won't be late.

DAVID: I saw some pumpkins for sale at the grocery store. I thought maybe I'd get a couple and we could carve them up. Make some cobwebs out of string. Cook a turkey. I thought we could do it up.

A little Halloween party.

GARBO: Well, I don't know –

DAVID: Stuff a sack, put a head on it, make it look like something scary, put it on the porch.

GARBO: A sack with a head? That does sound scary.

DAVID: I found a recipe for cranberry stuffing that sounds really good. And one with walnuts.

GARBO: Cranberries aren't really my thing.

DAVID: Well, like I said, there's one with walnuts, so –

GARBO: I should go. Henry's waiting.

DAVID: You've got some new (*referring to her wristbands*) ... what do you call them?

GARBO: I don't know. Wristbands, I guess.

DAVID: They're stylish. Like something you'd see in a magazine. Where did you – ?

GARBO: I made them.

DAVID: You – ?
Oh. The coon-skin cap.

GARBO: It was itchy, on my head. Hats aren't really –

DAVID: No. Well, they're not for everyone.

GARBO: I cut it up and sewed some snaps on it.

DAVID: You're crafty.

GARBO: You should lie down. You don't look well.

Garbo disappears.

SCENE THREE

DAVID: (*to audience*) That night I was sitting out back on the porch waiting for them, eating a Vachon brownie. Henry and Garbo had developed a small addiction to the manufactured cakes. There was a mixed box you could get at the grocery store with an assortment of pastries. Henry was partial to the ones with coconut sprinkles, and Garbo enjoyed a good cream filling.

The night was clear and there were stars in the sky.

The stars seemed to be hanging a bit lower in the sky than usual. Kind of drooping a bit.

I remembered being in a park late one night – this was a long time ago – and a friend of mine pointed up to a nondescript clump of stars and said, 'Look. Gemini. And there. Corniopus.'

Or something like Corniopus. I don't really remember. Cornicopius?

Anyway, so I remember I took my dick out of my pants and pissed in the dirt – it made a little pattern – and I pointed to it and said, 'Look, Angelica Houston.'

I don't know.

Building an entire belief system on a random pattern of stars.

Then again, I suppose bigger things have been built on less.

Henry and Garbo had been gone for hours. Longer than usual. I decided to go look for them. I thought they might enjoy a snack. I headed off into the forest with the box of Vachon cakes.

The ground was damp. Leaves stuck to my shoes and my pant legs. The dark made me dizzy and disoriented.

I realized I didn't really know where I was going.

I'll hear them singing, I thought. Their voices will take me to them.

I stood quietly and listened.

Nothing.

I unwrapped another Vachon brownie and put the wrapper in my pocket.

I noticed a small chipmunk lying in a fleck of light beside a tree. I often saw them lurking around the porch. Twitching around.

But this one was just kind of lounging, sprawled out on its back, its tongue hanging out of its mouth.

I threw a little chunk of the Vachon brownie at the chipmunk. It bounced on its head and stuck to the fur on its face.

It turned its head. It glanced in my direction.

I made a clapping sound. I nudged it with my foot.

It didn't move. It just stared back at me. Blurry-eyed.

A creeping feeling.

Something was there. In the trees. In the forest.

Something familiar.

The dark was faint. The stars droopy. The chipmunk aimless.

I shut my eyes.

What is that phrase? 'Everything catches up with you in time. You can run but you can't hide.'

I dropped the box of Vachon cakes on the ground.

I picked up a small rock. I walked over to the chipmunk and carefully placed the rock over its head.

It looked up at me.

I leaned over and brought all of my weight down onto the rock.

It crushed the chipmunk's head easily.

I dug a hole in the ground with the heel of my shoe. I buried the infected creature. I threw the rock into the trees.

Of course, my first thought was for them.

Henry and Garbo.

I started off deeper into the forest. I was walking in circles. Calling their names.

I was completely lost.

Eventually, my feet took me back to the cabin. Empty-handed.

I went inside and shut the doors and windows.

I climbed into bed. I was cold and damp.

I felt the cold creep out of me.

It lay down in bed beside me.

SCENE FOUR

Henry and Garbo appear. Garbo is holding a box of Vachon cakes.

HENRY: Hey.

DAVID: Mm?

HENRY: You okay?

DAVID: What?

HENRY: You were talking in your sleep.

DAVID: Was I?

HENRY: Banging around. You've got a bit of a gash on the side of your head.

DAVID: Oh, I –

HENRY: Some kind of nightmare maybe.

GARBO: Too many Vachon cakes before bed, probably. All that sugar.

HENRY: That's gonna turn into something. You should ice it.

DAVID: What?

HENRY: Your head.

DAVID: Oh, it's fine. It's –

GARBO: I don't think we have any ice.

DAVID: Where were you? I went to look for you but –

GARBO: I remember Henry putting bags of peas on my belly when I had pains. Frozen peas.

HENRY: I don't think we have any frozen vegetables on hand. But that's a good suggestion, Garbo.

DAVID: I'll just put some cold water on my face.

HENRY: Oh, wait a minute.

Henry disappears.
Garbo takes a Vachon cake out of the box and eats it.

DAVID: I think maybe I was just worried about you, out in the woods so late. I was worried that –

GARBO: Or the weather, the change of seasons. That can sometimes disturb people.

Henry reappears with a balloon.

HENRY: Voilà.

SCENE FIVE

DAVID: (*to audience*) Henry put a balloon full of cold water on my head. We had some balloons leftover from that Mexican picnic. Henry made an impromptu ice pack.

I lay back. Henry sat beside me on the bed. He pressed the balloon against the side of my head.

Garbo fell asleep in the chair in the corner of the room reading an entertainment magazine.

That night, in a dream, I saw them drifting away from me. I saw me left here alone. Unprotected.

When I woke up the next morning, my face was damp. There was water all over my pillow, and all over me.

The balloon had broken and was stuck to the side of my head. I peeled it off. Some of its colour stained onto my skin.

David disappears.

SCENE SIX

HENRY: Where's David?

GARBO: I don't know. I fell asleep.

HENRY: I hope he's all right.

GARBO: He was talking about getting some pumpkins. Yesterday, before we –

HENRY: Pumpkins?

GARBO: And cranberry stuffing.

HENRY: Cranberry stuffing. Wow.

Pause.

GARBO: I don't like cranberries.

HENRY: I thought you –

GARBO: No.

HENRY: Hm. Well. I'm gonna grab some Pop-Tarts. Have breakfast out in the hammock.

Henry and Garbo disappear.

SCENE SEVEN

David appears.

DAVID: (*to audience*) I drove into town. The morning was bright. I kept having flashes.

I kept seeing that dead chipmunk in my rear-view mirror, crawling out of the forest, onto the road, grabbing onto my bumper, pulling itself into my car, into the front seat and latching onto my face.

I tried to put it out of my mind. Maybe Garbo was right. The change of the seasons can put things out of whack.

The air was crisp. Henry and Garbo were home asleep in my bed. Everything was fine.

I took a deep breath.

I pulled into the parking lot of the grocery store. It was practically empty.

I bought a small turkey. The grocery store girl suggested one that came in a box. It was already cleaned and stuffed, so all you had to do was throw it in the oven. Three hundred and fifty degrees for five hours.

Outside, an older couple was sitting behind a picnic table full of pumpkins. They were wearing costumes and make-up. She was dressed like a hooker. He looked like some kind of pirate.

I picked out two medium-sized pumpkins. They helped me load them into my trunk.

I thanked them and congratulated them on their costumes. They said they weren't wearing costumes.

On the way home, I turned onto the main highway.

The rental agency that owned the cabin had a small office in a town nearby.

SCENE EIGHT

Henry and Garbo appear, holding two pumpkins.

GARBO: You –
    What?

DAVID: It's not finalized. I mean there's still paperwork and background checks, but I don't expect there to be any problems.

HENRY: This is big news. This is a surprise. You sneaky little –

DAVID: Well –

HENRY: How long have you been planning this?

DAVID: No, no, I wasn't –
    I mean, it was an impulse. I was buying the pumpkins and I thought, while I was at it, why not –

GARBO: How do you buy land? How do you do that?

DAVID: It's like anything else. It's a transaction. There are more things to sign but –

HENRY: You must have a nest egg. You must have a real bundle socked away.

DAVID: Well, I mean, you pay a bit now, you pay a bit later. Over time, it's manageable.

HENRY: Like a layaway plan.

DAVID: It didn't cost as much as you would think.

GARBO: I don't know what to think.

DAVID: This cabin is a bit out of the way, a bit remote. There wasn't much interest in the property, so –

HENRY: Does it come with the table? Does it come with the hammock?

DAVID: Yes, everything, they're throwing it all in.

HENRY: Well, wow. This is something. This is a big investment.

DAVID: Well, it's more than an investment. It's a home.

HENRY: A home? So –
You're gonna live here. You're gonna … ?

DAVID: Well, we. I mean –
I thought –

Pause.

GARBO: I'll go get some knives from the kitchen.
Henry, why don't you go put down some newspaper. Let's carve these things up.

Henry and Garbo disappear.

SCENE NINE

DAVID: (*to audience*) That night, by the fire, Henry and Garbo went at their pumpkins. I sat in a chair and watched them.
Henry used his knife like a paintbrush. Garbo used her knife like a weapon.
I put small candles inside the pumpkins.
I put them out on the porch. I sat outside and watched them flicker. Their faces made shadows on the trees and in the sky.
I stayed outside and kept an eye on the forest.
I told Henry and Garbo to stay inside and keep an eye on the turkey.

David disappears.

SCENE TEN

Henry and Garbo appear.

HENRY: I liked your pumpkin. I thought you did a good job on the eyes. I felt like it was really looking at me. It was spooky. Garbo? What's –

GARBO: I see you getting comfortable.

HENRY: What? I'm not –

GARBO: I see you getting attached.

HENRY: You're being paranoid.

GARBO: I see you in the hammock.

HENRY: Garbo –

GARBO: I see you with him.

HENRY: You and me. We're two peas in a pod.

GARBO: I see you –

A kitchen timer goes off.

HENRY: I better go check on that turkey.

Henry disappears.

GARBO: (*to audience*) Henry has a sympathetic nature. He falls into things, and people, easily. He has a lot to give and he doesn't expect much. That's a dangerous combination.
David was a leech. I could feel him. Sucking onto us. Prying. Invading. Like an infection.
So.

I had to protect us. I had to be the bitch. I didn't mind.

Out in the forest. Me and Henry. We'd disappear. Back into ourselves.

I'd put my head in Henry's lap. He'd sing to me. We'd make plans. Out in the forest. That's where we were who we were.

That's not something David could ever understand, or be a part of.

At night, out in the forest, that's where everything was … I don't know … safe and beautiful and familiar.

If David took that away, or upset that, I would split his fucking –

A kitchen timer goes off. David appears.

GARBO: Jesus –

DAVID: I thought I heard the kitchen timer go off.

GARBO: Jesus. Don't sneak up on me. Don't do that.

Pause.

DAVID: How's that bird doing?

GARBO: Henry went to check on it.

DAVID: Maybe you should help him. Four hands are better than two.

Garbo disappears.

SCENE ELEVEN

DAVID: (*to audience*) Things started happening.

Things that couldn't be ignored.

The forest seemed to be withering. The trees, the branches, were becoming flaccid and limp. The colour was draining out of the leaves, seeping into the ground and disappearing. The wind, which used to howl through the forest, now just kind of made small sputtering sounds, like a cough.

Henry and Garbo were becoming more and more distant. Almost every night. The two of them. Out into the forest.

I tried to discourage them from going outside, but they would kind of put me off. Especially Garbo.

Inside the cabin, doors were closed more than they were open.

Whispers replaced songs.

Garbo wasn't eating. I would cook up some braised ribs or a platter of fajitas. She would push the food away or just sit and look at it. Kind of sneering at it.

Henry was spending more and more time in the hammock. He would lie out there, his big hooded sweater pulled over his face, rocking back and forth, drumming to himself, lost somewhere.

Henry and Garbo appear in the distance.

I felt it. Creeping in. Through cracks. Out of the forest. Into the cabin. Back into my life.

GARBO: If you're going into town maybe you could pick us up a couple of parkas.

DAVID: What? Parkas?

GARBO: Thick winter coats.

DAVID: Yes, I know what parkas are, but –

GARBO: I think we saw some snowflakes the other night.

DAVID: You spend too much time out there, in the woods, in the cold. You're going to catch something. You should stay here. I hardly see you anymore, and –

You're not looking well, either of you. Henry, you've lost colour in your face, and Garbo, you're not eating –

GARBO: You worry too much.

DAVID: Maybe there are things to worry about, maybe there are things I know that you don't know and –

Pause.

HENRY: The new songs are really coming along. I think we're onto something. We're working with a bit of a reggae style. I'm getting pretty tight on the drums. I think you're gonna be impressed.

DAVID: Yes, I'd like to hear something because, I mean, I haven't heard much lately. You've been –

HENRY: We've been saving it. We want to surprise you.

Pause.

DAVID: I thought we could get up early tomorrow. Have a brunch-type thing. Stay in. Make some waffles.

GARBO: Waffles?

DAVID: That new waffle iron I bought a while ago, you know, get some use out of it. I'll dig it out of the back of the closet. I'll pick up some fresh fruit. I think that apple stand down the road might still be open.

GARBO: Oh, I don't know about waffles.

DAVID: Some cinnamon waffles.

GARBO: I think waffles are a bit heavy, first thing in the morning. I wouldn't bother.

DAVID: It's no bother.

GARBO: I'm just saying –

DAVID: It's no bother.

Henry and Garbo disappear.

SCENE TWELVE

DAVID: (*to audience*) There was a small farm about five kilometres down the road, before you reach the apple stand. A hobby farm. A long laneway. A big front lawn.

The front lawn was strewn with household items and old farm equipment. All sprawled out, randomly. Some kind of estate sale. A moving sale.

A little kid was sitting behind a miniature plastic table on a miniature plastic lawn chair.

He was wearing a puffy coat.

'I know you,' I said.

He didn't look up. He was opening and closing a small hook on the plastic money box.

'Remember? The midnight concert in the woods. I kneed you in the belly.'

He snapped the box tight. He looked at the ground. 'You gonna buy something?'

He sounded like he was hauling his words up a cliff.

I picked up some kind of metal jaw-type thing and examined it. I had no idea what it was.

And then, there, sandwiched between some dishes.

My waffle iron.

The woman came over and stood behind the kid.

'Barely used,' she said. 'Got it second-hand. Coupla teenagers selling stuff for quick cash. Saving up, they said. For a little getaway.'

I looked around and saw my Crock-Pot, which I used once to make a slow-cooking stew; my pasta-maker; my croquet set; my blender; and my game of Monopoly.

'Make me an offer.'

She threw everything into a wooden crate with some other odds and ends: a macramé wall clock, a paper-towel rack, a couple of large rusty chains, a tin of heavy nails, old tools and some leather collars that had once been used for securing a couple of frisky dogs that were now dead.

SCENE THIRTEEN

Henry and Garbo appear with a platter of waffles.

HENRY: These are –

DAVID: I was hoping for some fresh apples to put on top. But it was closed up.
    Everything around here seems to be closing up.

HENRY: Well, they're really spicy.

DAVID: It's the cinnamon.

GARBO: Mm.

DAVID: You don't think they're too heavy?

HENRY: What? No.

DAVID: Because Garbo thought they might be too heavy first thing in the morning. Isn't that what you said?

GARBO: Once in a while they're not so bad. I'll probably skip lunch.

DAVID: The waffle iron is still hot. I'll whip up a fresh batch.

David disappears.

HENRY: (*to audience*) We went through about four platters of waffles. We'd finish them off and David would be back in the kitchen, over the grill. He stood and watched us eat. He didn't take a bite.

He didn't say much. The maple syrup stung our teeth and gave us cramps. Garbo threw up in her napkin but continued eating. Every guilty bite. He never mentioned the waffle iron. Neither did we.

GARBO: (*to audience*) Things were getting more and more tense. He started behaving oddly. I mean, more oddly. We noticed things.

HENRY: (*to audience*) He rarely left the cabin. He was always sneaking around, locking doors and windows. Always watching us from corners. Or standing on the porch, staring out at the forest.

GARBO: (*to audience*) We could hear him mumbling in his sleep. Talking about some kind of sickness and infected people.

HENRY: (*to audience*) We started finding pieces of us hidden away. In closets or cupboards. Buried outside under piles of leaves. Hanging from trees at the edge of the forest. Our leftover food, our unwashed clothes, our scribbled notes. All wrapped up kind of … delicately.

GARBO: (*to audience*) I saw our names carved into the wooden table. Big shaky letters.

HENRY: (*to audience*) Garbo was getting paranoid and anxious.

GARBO: (*to audience*) I told Henry, 'Things don't happen without planning.'
    We started hoarding things away: food, clothing, gear, money. We had saved up about $300 from selling David's stuff. And from stealing a bit.
    Not much, but something.
    There was a place deep in the woods. A hollow tree. It was big and dry. We piled everything up inside of it.

David appears with a platter of waffles.

DAVID: Finished?

HENRY: I think we ate enough waffles to feed a Belgian army. They're popular in Belgium. Belgian waffles.

DAVID: Yes. And in Switzerland too, I think.

HENRY: Although I don't think there's such a thing as Swiss waffles. Are there?

Pause.

GARBO: I'll just wash this up. Henry why don't you come and help me?

Garbo disappears with the platter.

HENRY: Well. That was – Those waffles had a real kick to them. The cinnamon. It was spicy.

Henry disappears.

SCENE FOURTEEN

DAVID: (*to audience*) Henry and Garbo went into the kitchen. I went outside onto the porch.
    The forest loomed in front of me. It was an open mouth. I felt like I was being swallowed.
    I grabbed onto the porch railing.
    I could see Henry and Garbo through the kitchen window. They were over the sink. Garbo was washing the platter and the utensils. Henry was scrubbing the waffle iron with a Brillo pad.
    I had to do something, because, I mean –
    You have to understand.
    When you find something safe, when you find something beautiful, you have to hold onto it, you have to take care of it, you have to protect it, whatever the cost.

David disappears.

SCENE FIFTEEN

Henry and Garbo appear.

GARBO: Henry. Look at me. Henry. It's time. No more games. Henry –

HENRY: One last performance. In the woods. An act of breathtaking magnitude. Then, *poof!*

Henry and Garbo disappear.

SCENE SIXTEEN

David appears, holding Garbo's stick.

DAVID: (*to audience*) The next few days were very quiet.

Henry and Garbo started sleeping by the fire in the main room. Garbo had developed a recurring cough. She said she didn't want to keep me awake at night.

Lying in my bed at night, alone, I started thinking about the city, and the people I used to know, and the things I lost.

I remembered my friend. Who started the collage circle. Who wore the coon-skin cap. Who was dead.

I remembered her burial.

I remembered sitting outside on a white plastic chair, under a tree, in the wind. I remembered a large pile of dirt, and a large hole, and a yellow hydraulic-type thing they used to lower the casket into the ground.

It made a horrible clicking sound.

A person sitting next to me took my hand and whispered, 'Well, after all is said and done, we still have our memories.'

And I remember thinking, watching the casket drop into the ground, I remember thinking, 'Well, that's a real comfort.'

I mean, what are they? Memories. What do they do? What purpose do they serve, really?

I always thought of them as little scabs all over my body

that I would pick at and pick at until they bled and inevitably caused me great pain and loneliness.

Henry and Garbo appear.

HENRY: We have something for you.

Henry gives David a small homemade card.

DAVID: Well –

HENRY: It's an invitation.

DAVID: It is. It looks very official. The lettering …

GARBO: That's Henry. He's crafty.

DAVID: It's really good. It's almost like calligraphy.

HENRY: Well, I don't know about calligraphy, but – I tried to make it look –

DAVID: (*reading*) Henry and Garbo. Tomorrow night. Midnight. Behind the porch.

HENRY: The wording could be better, I think.

DAVID: It's very clear.

HENRY: We've been working hard on it, so …

DAVID: The invitation?

HENRY: The music.

DAVID: Yes, all that work. All those nights out in the forest.

HENRY: I think you'll be impressed.

DAVID: A private performance.

HENRY: For you.

DAVID: For me?

HENRY: Just for you.

DAVID: Well, that's –
I mean –
This is –
Should I dress up?

GARBO: Well, it's outside, so –

DAVID: (*reading the invitation*) Right. Behind the porch.

GARBO: So you'll have to dress warmly. A coat and maybe some gloves. It's cold at night.

DAVID: We could have some wine, and maybe some nibblies?

HENRY: Nibblies?

DAVID: Little snacks. We could put them on a tray and have a little party. A post-show reception.

HENRY: Don't go to any trouble.

DAVID: All your hard work.

GARBO: We thought we'd preview it for you, you know, before we ...

Pause.

DAVID: Before you ... ?

GARBO: Oh, you know.

Pause.

HENRY: Garbo made some pasta for dinner. It's from a package, but –

DAVID: Oh, that's –

HENRY: Not like your fancy stuff, but –

DAVID: There's nothing wrong with packages.

HENRY: What was that thing you made? Ravioli?

DAVID: Cannelloni.

HENRY: Right. You stuffed it with something.

DAVID: Ricotta cheese.

HENRY: Ricotta cheese.

GARBO: Well, this isn't ricotta cheese, but.

HENRY: We're going to eat it, so …

DAVID: Well. I think we've got some napkins leftover from Halloween. I'll see if I can dig them up.

David starts to leave.

HENRY: You're really attached to that.

DAVID: What?

HENRY: That stick.

DAVID: Oh. Yes.

HENRY: You're gonna make us jealous.

DAVID: Well, I've been thinking about what I could do with it, and I was thinking –

HENRY: You could strip it. Clean it up a bit. Mount it on the wall over the fireplace.

DAVID: Well, I don't know if I could do that. I haven't got your touch with wood, but I was thinking –

HENRY: It's a nice stick. It would look nice on a wall.

DAVID: Well, that's Garbo. I mean, she found it.

GARBO: Well, I saw it and I thought of you.

HENRY: See? It's you. Beautiful things come your way.

DAVID: Well, I don't know about that –

HENRY: We came your way, didn't we?

DAVID: Yes, you did.

David disappears.

SCENE SEVENTEEN

GARBO: (*to audience*) We packed up everything we had and stored it inside the tree.

It was hard work, getting all our things into those old knapsacks. It's amazing how much stuff we acquired over the months: a harmonica, a hatchet, sleeping bags, wool socks, some magazines, a portable radio.

We should have asked David to buy us some bigger knapsacks, or a duffle bag. But I mean, you can't think of everything.

I packed it all up while Henry made a small stage out of

wood behind the porch. He was going all out. He was making a real effort.

It was important to him, for some reason. This game. This act.

I couldn't really give a shit. You have to understand. I'm not a heartless bitch. But I mean …

This wasn't our life. This wasn't us.

A hammock. A quilt. Homemade cannelloni.

This was nothing.

Everything's temporary.

You live your life depending on things, you lose. That's what I think.

Me and Henry.

We were always peeking around corners.

We were hopeful, wandering spirits.

SCENE EIGHTEEN

Henry appears.

HENRY: (*to audience*) I made a small stage out of wood behind the porch. Some logs. Some boards.

Some leaves and branches for decoration. I put tea lights around the stage and on the porch. It wasn't much, but it was something. It took me all day. I was tired.

I was wearing my heavy sweater, so I was sweating a bit. I lay down in the hammock. I swung back and forth. I was drumming to myself.

Going over things. In my head. The act. The music.

And other things. The Mexican picnic. The bathtub. The quilts. The fireplace. The cereal.

For a moment I saw us staying here. I imagined what it could be like. Winter would come. I'd learn to hunt. We'd play music on the porch. Garbo would make clothes. David would cook food. I'd grow a beard.

Time would pass but we wouldn't feel it passing.

For a moment. I saw the possibility. Of this.

Pause.

I looked back at the cabin. They were both watching me. Garbo was standing in the window. She was wrapped up in the quilt. David was standing in the doorway. He was tapping the floor with Garbo's stick. He motioned at me to come inside. I went inside. He shut the door.

It felt colder inside than it did outside. The fire wasn't really going. It was just kind of smouldering. A few tiny flames. Wafts of smoke filling up the cabin.

Garbo came over and swallowed me up in the quilt. We sat down in front of the fireplace.

David suggested a little nap. To refresh ourselves. Before the performance.

I told him to wake us up in a few hours.

He stood over us.

I looked up at him.

There was something in his eyes I couldn't understand.

Me and Garbo were out like a light.

SCENE NINETEEN

David appears, still holding the stick.

DAVID: (*to audience*) The two of them were curled up together.

They fell asleep almost immediately after their heads hit the floor. The poor things. They were worn out.

Henry's small mouth was open slightly and Garbo's arm was lying across his chest.

I was above them. I tried to see them as I first saw them. Lying on the ground outside the grocery store. Their faces lit up. Their eyelids flickering. I tried to remember.

But everything was blurry.

Smoke was wafting around the cabin. My eyes started watering.

I raised up the stick.

I didn't know what to aim at. Their foreheads? Their chests?

I decided I would strike Henry first.

And then I thought, 'Okay, the forehead.'

I was about to bring it down when suddenly I stopped. I thought, 'What am I doing? This isn't me. I can't do this.'

I placed the stick beside the fireplace and walked away.

I sat in a chair, shaking a bit.

I looked around the cabin, looking for something. I didn't know what I was looking for.

The table, the rug, a few chairs. In the bedroom: a large bed, a pile of magazines, Henry's homemade canoe. In the kitchen: a fridge, some dishes, a bread knife, a toaster, a gas stove.

A gas stove.

I sealed off the doors and windows with tea towels, winter scarves and bedsheets. I blew out the pilot light. I turned on the gas.

I went outside onto the porch.

I waited patiently for the cabin to fill up with gas.

I watched through the window, shivering.

I could see Henry and Garbo squirming a bit, moving their bodies around together, under the quilt, taking in the gas.

It seemed to take forever.

Eventually, they became completely still.

Garbo's arm fell off Henry's chest and dropped to the floor.

SCENE TWENTY

Henry and Garbo appear, in the distance. Garbo's head is in Henry's lap.

HENRY: Garbo?

GARBO: Mm?

HENRY: Can you – ?

GARBO: What?

HENRY: Just sit still. Just –

GARBO: I am.

HENRY: You're fidgeting. You're always –

GARBO: The ground is wet. I'm sitting on a rock.

HENRY: Just – Just relax.

Pause.

GARBO: Oh, I want to tell you something. I was reading this celebrity interview in a magazine with this actress.

HENRY: Hm.

GARBO: And the interviewer said to her, 'So, how are you these days?' And she said, 'My soul is at peace and my heart is devout.'

HENRY: My soul is … what?

GARBO: My soul is at peace and my heart is devout.

HENRY: Hm, that's …

Pause.

GARBO: Henry?

Henry and Garbo remain in a hazy light.

SCENE TWENTY-ONE

DAVID: (*to audience*) I dragged them outside. They were dead weight. Their bodies and faces were droopy. I pulled the wooden crate out from under the porch. The one I got from the moving sale.

I rummaged through it. I dug out the leather collars, the heavy chains and some nails.

I put the leather collars around their necks. I attached the chains to the collars. I nailed the chains to the porch.

I sat down wrapped in a quilt and I watched them.

They didn't move.

I lit the tea lights.

Still, they weren't moving.

I hoped that I hadn't left them in the cabin too long in the gas. I'm not a chemist or an engineer or anything like that.

The moon was high in the sky and it was incredibly bright. It shone on their faces and their faces reflected onto the trees and into the sky. It was –

GARBO: Henry? Henry?

DAVID: (*to audience*) Garbo started coughing and squirming around a bit. Henry didn't move.

GARBO: (*to David*) What did you do? What did you –

DAVID: (*to audience*) I didn't really know what to say at that point. I wanted to say, 'It's going to be okay.' That they were safe now. But I didn't. I couldn't say anything.

GARBO: Henry? Henry? (*to David*) What did you do?

DAVID: (*to audience*) I thought, 'Eventually, I'll tell them. I'll tell them about the world I knew and the people I lost. And they'll understand.'

GARBO: Henry?

DAVID: But right then I wanted Garbo to be quiet. I wanted Henry to get up. I wanted to hear them sing.

GARBO: Henry, get up. Henry, get up. Breathe. Move. Henry.

DAVID: (*to audience*) I watched Henry and Garbo's shadows dance across the forest, their faces pressed against the trees, their eyes hovering in the sky. And I felt safe. I felt protected. We were here. We were together. The three of us. Together. We could save each other.

GARBO: (*to David*) What did you do? What did you do – ?

THE END

RECOVERY

Recovery was commissioned and first produced by the National Arts Center in Ottawa in April 2006.

Ben: Ian Leung
Clare: Kate Hurman
Ash: John Koengsen
Leroy: Jeff Lawson
Mya: Alix Sideris
Alex: Paul Wernick

Director: David Oiye
Set and costume design: Kim Nielson
Lighting design: David Fraser
Original music and sound design: Robert Perrault
Stage Manager: Stephanie Seguin
Dramaturge: Lise Ann Johnson

It has since been produced by Rumble Theatre (Vancouver, BC) and the University of Toledo's School of Theatre and Film (Ohio, USA).

My thanks to the National Arts Centre, Playwrights' Workshop Montreal, the 2004 Banff playRites Colony and the many directors, actors and designers across the country who have contributed to this script.

CHARACTERS

Ben (*thirties*)
Clare (*thirties*)
Ash (*sixties*)
Leroy (*twenties*)
Mya (*twenties*)
Alex (*twelve*)

PRODUCTION NOTES

Although the play has very few stage directions, it should still have a strong physical, auditory and visual quality.

The use of slides, projections, video, holograms, recorded voices, sound effects and children are encouraged.

Image – Oping & Scene 2 stimulate image
ny oping of No Exit / Sartre.

'Let me be weak, let me sleep, and dream of sheep.'
– Kate Bush

PART ONE

SCENE ONE

BEN: In a banquet room at a hotel downtown they offer us warm croissants and espresso. They give us brochures and show us slides. Pictures of rotting teeth, infected skin and a man lying on a cot, emaciated. Pictures of people wandering naked down streets. Pictures of bodies lying dead in alleys, unattended, floating in pools of water, grey and bloated, people poking them with sticks and mothers holding dead, limp children.

They say, 'This isn't happening yet, but it could happen.' They say, 'It's not a question of if, it's a question of when.' They say, 'You may not think you have a problem, but that's often the first sign you have a problem.' They say, 'If you love yourself or there's someone you love.'

I sign a release form and give them a series of cheques. The next day my mother and I take a limousine to the airport. I get on a chartered flight. I am allowed to bring one piece of luggage. Just the essentials: toiletries, clothing. Personal items – photographs, stuffed animals, CDs, jewellery – aren't encouraged.

'Everything will be waiting for you when you come home.'

SCENE TWO

CLARE: You probably have a lot of questions. How was the travel?

BEN: Planes I find disorienting. You get on, you're somewhere. You get off, you're somewhere else. It's jarring.

CLARE: Yes, and the seating is often cramped, and the recycled air. Although you can buy your own vials of oxygen now, so ...

BEN: There was a large person beside me who was constantly shifting back and forth like a –

Well, constantly fidgeting. I requested another seat, and luckily there were a few empty seats on the plane, but even still the attendant gave me a condescending look.

CLARE: There are some people who don't enjoy doing things for others, even if it costs them nothing.

BEN: Regardless –

CLARE: Here you are, in one piece.

BEN: When we were landing, I thought I saw some penguins.

CLARE: Yes, they like to flop about on the coastline.

BEN: Well, that's something.

CLARE: Some of the Residents will get a little adventurous, plan a little expedition, pack a lunch, make a day of it, out to the coast with the penguins. It's not encouraged, but –

BEN: Are they friendly?

CLARE: Well, they're not unfriendly. I wouldn't want one for a pet, I don't think.

BEN: No, I wouldn't imagine.

CLARE: Some of the Residents, on the other hand ...

BEN: I beg your pardon?

CLARE: Oh, I was making a joke.

BEN: I'm sorry, I don't understand.

CLARE: Well, perhaps now is not the best time for — You're probably feeling a bit fuzzy.

BEN: A bit, yes.

CLARE: Now that you're here –

BEN: What did you say? Fuzzy, but …

CLARE: It's an adjustment, but I think you'll find it can be fun, it can be an adventure.

BEN: I mean, you hear so many contradictory things these days from so many people. Do this, try that.

CLARE: You've made a good choice. We're a relatively new outfit, but I think we're making a lot of progress.

BEN: Yes, well, it was either this one, or there was one off the coast of Japan that sounded –

CLARE: That's a popular spot.

BEN: I thought it sounded exotic, but in the end –

CLARE: No penguins, of course, but lots of bamboo, if that's your thing.

BEN: I saw your advertisements on the television, the celebrity endorsements, and I thought –

CLARE: We've received some nice exposure over the past few months.

BEN: I thought, if it's good enough for John Stamos –

CLARE: He has such an honest quality to him, don't you think?

BEN: And your treatment sounded –

CLARE: We're working primarily with ventilation.

BEN: I have a funny taste at the back of my mouth.

CLARE: You'll get used to that.

BEN: It wasn't easy getting a spot. There was a waiting list but my mother pulled some strings so they managed to squeeze me in.

CLARE: We have close to 5,000 people staying with us.

BEN: Wow, that's –

CLARE: It's all very well organized, so you shouldn't feel too over-whelmed by it all. We've tried to make it as intimate and homey as possible, little personal touches here and there.

BEN: Yes, I saw the large Chinese vases and the small marble tables in the corridors, and I think they're really –

CLARE: There are ten wings or arms – separate little communities really – each with their own restaurant, and a games room, and a sunshine room, and an exercise room with blue mats, and a music room with some instruments –

BEN: I used to play in a chamber quartet.

CLARE: Really?

BEN: Yes, the violin.

CLARE: Well, I don't know about violins. I think we have some recorders, a xylophone, a few trombones, a tambourine. You know, odds and ends.

BEN: That would be funny.

CLARE: What's that?

BEN: Oh, I was just imagining the musical possibilities, the combi-nation of those instruments all thrown together.

CLARE: Yes, that would be funny.

BEN: I'm sorry, I feel as though I should lie down.

CLARE: I just wanted to make sure everything was okey-dokey.

BEN: Everyone has been very helpful and generous. It will probably take me a few days to get a sense of the place.

CLARE: It's a complicated system at first, but in the end I think you'll find it makes some kind of sense.

BEN: I haven't heard that expression in a long time.

CLARE: What's that?

BEN: Okey-dokey.

CLARE: Oh, my son has taken it up. I don't know where he got it. You can find you own way to your room?

BEN: I'm in the Woodpecker Wing, so that's … ?

CLARE: Just down two flights and then straight ahead on your left.

BEN: Yes, I think I can remember that.

CLARE: Well, sweet dreams.

SCENE THREE

BEN: The first night, it's uncomfortable. Everything feels strange. I unpack. I arrange things in my room, flicking light switches, looking at the floor tiles, arranging hangers, keeping myself occupied. I lie on top of the bed. The bedspread is synthetic and has a green kind of jungle pattern on it.

The sound of a violin.
A woman and a boy appear.

BEN: I think of my mother at the airport. At the gate, waving good-bye, wearing a long coat, short white gloves and a mink stole. She was of that pedigree where just leaving the house was a formal occasion.

She gave me a card with a black-and-white photograph of a young boy holding a violin. When you open the card, it plays a little melody. The boy moves around, his little arms and his little fingers, like he's actually playing the violin. Inside it says, 'Thinking of You.'

My mother.

I imagine she spent a lot of time picking that card out. It's certainly not something I would have picked out for myself, but ... I put it on the small desk, facing me.

Looking around the room, I think to myself, 'Do we create meaning out of the things in our lives, or do the things in our lives create meaning?'

Later in the night, my head starts to ache, my lungs start to itch, my body – my bowels, my stomach – start to tighten and convulse.

I put on my housecoat and go to the bathroom –

SCENE FOUR

ASH: Oh, I'm sorry, are you ... ?

BEN: Oh, no –

ASH: I can come back.

BEN: No, it's fine. I'm not really used to sharing a bathroom. It's been a long time since –

ASH: Well, there are always sacrifices that have to be made in these situations. There's plenty of cabinet space, at least.

BEN: The bedrooms are nice. Not extravagant, but, you know, a small rug, a bedspread, a lamp, a desk. The lamp I find a bit bright, but I threw a scarf over it and now it's fine.

ASH: I hung some fabric on my wall for a bit of colour and texture. I enjoy a bit of –

BEN: Sorry, so how many share this bathroom exactly?

ASH: There are three of us.

BEN: Right. I don't mean to harp on it, but as I've said, it's been a long time since I've shared a bathroom.

ASH: Yes, well, you get used to it.

BEN: Sometimes things – sounds – come out of you that you would rather keep to yourself.

ASH: We're all in the same boat.

BEN: Yes.

ASH: Anyway, it's all quite soundproof.

BEN: That's good.

ASH: They're cleaned every day as well.

BEN: Yes, I saw them with their carts and uniforms, up and down the corridors. They seem very conscientious.

ASH: I've stayed in hotels with far worse service.

BEN: I'd be interested in going out to see some of those penguins. I've heard sometimes little expeditions are planned …

ASH: Those have been temporarily suspended, I'm afraid.

BEN: Oh, that's too bad.

ASH: Yes, a young boy got snatched up by one of the penguins and —

BEN: Jesus.

ASH: Right down into the water.

BEN: I didn't realize they could be so aggressive.

ASH: As you can imagine, he didn't have much of a chance.

BEN: No, not in those conditions. The water must have been –

ASH: So, out of respect –

BEN: Yes, of course.

ASH: But I've heard there's a ping-pong tournament being planned.

BEN: I'm really not one for competitive sports.

ASH: There's going to be a small memorial service for the poor boy.

BEN: Did they recover his ... um...

ASH: Oh, no. Perhaps the penguins took care of it. I'm not really sure what they do with their dead – penguins – but perhaps some of the older penguins buried him or gave him a send off. I really don't know.

> Regardless, a few of us are getting together to say a few words.

> He has no family here, so ...

BEN: Well, let me know.

ASH: On Thursday, in the Elephant Room.

BEN: The Elephant Room?

ASH: You get used to the funny little names of things. They actually come in handy, as this can be a confusing place.

BEN: Yes, it's very large. *(pause)* I'm sorry.

ASH: The diarrhea should stop after a few days. Your body will adjust and then you'll just experience some fuzziness the odd time.

BEN: Yes, that's what I was told to expect.

ASH: It's a good place, though. Comfortable. Please feel free to move some of my toiletries around to make some space.

BEN: Oh no, there's plenty of room. I don't have much.

ASH: As you can see I've lots of shampoo and conditioner if you ever run short. *Is he bald?*

BEN: That's kind, thank you. I don't really use conditioner, but thank you.

SCENE FIVE

BEN: The bathroom I share with Ash, a man in his sixties, and Leroy, a young German teenager who mainly keeps to himself, or perhaps just doesn't speak English.

LEROY: I'm actually from Amsterdam and I speak English fine. I'm not a teenager, I'm twenty-four. I come from a small, tightly knit family. I have a younger sister named Joan. My parents are cultural attachés. We host a lot of dinner parties. When I was a child, I shared a fondue with Nina Simone and Ute Lemper. I speak German as well.

BEN: Ash is very tidy and considerate. He's been here about three weeks. We often eat our meals together. Sometimes, after dinner, we go for walks around the Complex, exploring, peeking in rooms, opening doors, sneaking around like a couple of school girls.

ASH: I've always been a curious person. When I was a child, I was always putting things into my mouth. I enjoy foreign films from obscure countries. On vacations, I always search out local bars, eat local dishes and play with local children.

My friends, Jack and Harold – people used to call us the three sisters – we used to terrorize the city, going to all the newest clubs, listening to all the newest music, wearing all the newest styles of jeans.

BEN: You certainly wouldn't put the three of us in a lineup and say, 'Well, they go together.'

ASH: I have a small exclusive firm that designs and manufactures wooden furniture. Mainly chairs, but also some small low tables. I've done quite well for myself. One of my chairs was actually bought by Sting and his wife Trudie, and another by Victoria and David Beckham.

LEROY: I work as an intern for a European music magazine. I get to travel a lot, getting stories, interviews, going to clubs.

Doing a story in Copenhagen I sat in on a recording session with the Windsor Concert Party, an electronic music collective from Montreal, and got to do some backup vocals – a kind of high-pitched shrieking – and later that night had very interesting sex with a young Norwegian singer.

BEN: But you know, at the end of the day, there's the one thing we all have in common, the tidy old man, the surly German teenager, and me, and thousands and thousands and thousands of others. The one thing that links us all –

ASH: What is that dramatic expression? 'The turning point,' or 'the point of no return' –

The sound of a chamber quartet.

BEN: I was at a garden party. My chamber quartet had been booked to play an event for this particularly mediocre but well-publicized visual artist. We were positioned under a large maple tree –

ASH: *The Turning Point* is, of course, that classic film with Shirley MacLaine and Anne Bancroft. But I don't know if that's relevant.

BEN: Maple keys kept falling into my hair, and there was a teenager who sat cross-legged on the lawn in front of us who kept throwing little pieces of shrimp at me and was giving me a small erection.

During a break, the caterers brought out a white ceramic tray with some odd-looking snacks on it. I'd never seen anything like them before.

ASH: At first, I thought they were meant to be decorative, something you put on a plate or maybe string together for a chunky necklace. Jack and Harold brought a bag of them over one morning. We were going to an early showing of a film that starred a young actor we all enjoyed. They came across them at the back of a health food store in Little India. It was all very subversive.

LEROY: No one is content when they're young. The pressure to be original is like a … what is it … like a vice grip on your balls. As soon as someone has what you have, it is no longer valuable. You spend your life keeping up, looking for new things to do, new things to say, new things to try.

BEN: The hosts of the party had come across them during a vacation in London. They were passing them around with champagne to the guests, and offered us some as well.

LEROY: I got an email. One of those bulk things – you know, herbal remedies, penis extensions, discount cancer drugs. The email said, 'This is what you crave.'

BEN: Most people at the party seemed to know about this new fad, and they became very quiet and tight, shifting back and forth. After the champagne, everyone dug in.

LEROY: It had a hard outer shell with a small blue insignia on it – a fish or a dolphin or something. You cracked open the shell and –

ASH: We ate the entire batch in one go, me, Harold and Jack. We never made it to the film. Instead, we put on some African music and danced outside on my balcony.

BEN: I remember chasing that teenager around the lawn with my violin, the viola player and the cellist floating face up in the pool.

LEROY: Pretty soon, everyone I knew was talking about this new product. Underground things don't stay underground for very long.

BEN: No one really knew where it came from.

ASH: Everyone had a theory, but it was always, you know, a friend of a friend heard this or that.

LEROY: I heard something about a traditional Mexican plant.

BEN: There were rumours it was originally developed as a vitamin supplement for dogs.

ASH: I pictured a vast orchard with small, twisting trees and shirt-less Portuguese workers with baskets tied to their waists.

LEROY: Soon, it started was popping up everywhere: in clubs, in parks, at sporting events, daycare centres.

BEN: And then came the warnings, the full-page articles in the newspapers.

LEROY: The billboards, the pull-out sections in magazines, the investigative news programs.

ASH: The symptoms, the panic, the fear.

BEN: People started going away.

ASH: Jack and Harold drove me to the airport. They gave me a blue mitten-and-scarf set. They were waiting to get into a centre in Florida. They bought themselves matching Speedos and swimming goggles.

LEROY: The night before I was sent away, my parents cooked lamb, my little sister made a paper hat and I went out and had sex with a Russian prostitute. I came home late, I locked myself in my room and played loud music. My parents knocked on my bedroom door.

They said, 'For God's sake, kids your age go to war, live under a tarp and get shot in the head, and they do this voluntarily, so I mean, I don't know why you're pulling a face. We're trying to help you.'

They gave me a brown leather notebook and a black pen. 'For your personal thoughts,' they said.

SCENE SIX

BEN: Ash?

ASH: Ben –

BEN: It's late. What are you –

ASH: Come with me. I have a surprise for you.

BEN: Ash pulls me out of the room. He drags me down a long corridor, around a corner, through a small door.

ASH: Sh.

BEN: Where are we?

ASH: This way.

BEN: We go up a long, steep, narrow staircase. It's dark and musty. I feel dizzy and out of breath.

ASH: Give me your hand.

BEN: At the top of the staircase, another small door. Ash pushes it open and we crawl inside. A large circular room enclosed in clear glass high above the ground. Everything is covered in dust. The moon reflects in the windows. A hazy glow. In the centre of the room, there's a large, bulky-looking telescope.

ASH: This place must have been an old research station. The telescope is still in good working condition.

BEN: I find that hard to believe. The eyepiece is cracked and there's a heavy build-up of rust. I can't see anything through the lens but clouds and foggy shapes.

ASH: You're not using it properly.

BEN: It's a telescope. You look. You see.

ASH: You interpret.

BEN: Anyway, he's older and his voice sounds assured, so I suppose he might know what he's talking about.

ASH: Out there, beside the small cliff.

BEN: He puts his hands on my waist. He leans in behind me and turns my body.

ASH: Look, there.

BEN: I'm sorry, I can't see anything,

ASH: Out there, look.

BEN: I don't know what I'm supposed to be looking at.

ASH: The penguins.

BEN: The penguins?

ASH: You wanted to see the penguins.

BEN: Yes, I did, but –

ASH: There they are.

BEN: Um –

ASH: It's not, you know, in the flesh, but at least you can see –

BEN: I'm sorry, I can't –

ASH: Their little beaks, their little feet, their little flippers.

BEN: I'm afraid I'm not seeing what you're seeing.

ASH: For God's sake, are you blind? Right there.

BEN: Ash nudges me out of the way.

ASH: Look at them. Look at them waddling. Is that the right word? Waddling?

BEN: He starts giggling to himself.

ASH: Look at them.

BEN: I'll leave you and the penguins alone then.

ASH: By the way, I signed you up for that ping-pong tournament.

BEN: You sneaky bastard.

ASH: Jesus Christ, look at them.

SCENE SEVEN

BEN: I head back downstairs to the bathroom to wash up. Leroy appears in the doorway in boxer shorts, with a towel around his neck.

LEROY: Are you finished?

BEN: Oh, hello. I'm sorry. I didn't know you spoke English.

LEROY: Yup.

BEN: Someone told me you were German.

LEROY: Who told you I was German?

BEN: I don't know, maybe I just made it up, or thought –

LEROY: I'm from Amsterdam.

BEN: I've never been.

LEROY: Well, we speak Dutch there.

BEN: Oh, I know. I'm afraid English is my only –

LEROY: Yes, English people tend to speak English and that's about it.

BEN: I can read music, but I guess that's not really a language, per se. Although some people might consider music a kind of –

LEROY: So, I've got to pee.

SCENE EIGHT

BEN: Leroy isn't going to win any personality contests, which is fine. He pretty much keeps to himself.

Sometimes, in the bathroom, we all cross paths. Ash will try to start a conversation. He'll say something like 'hello' or 'excuse me.' Leroy will tense up, grind his teeth and kind of snort.

ASH: 'Look at me,' I say to myself. 'Sharing a bathroom with a twenty-four year old Dutch boy.' And then I say to myself, 'Look at me, sharing a bathroom with a twenty-four-year-old Dutch boy.'

BEN: During meals, Leroy always sits on his own, his head buried in his food.

LEROY: I don't like people watching me eat. I don't like having to watch other people eat.

Mya appears.

BEN: There's a brown-haired girl who works at the restaurant who seems to be taken with our sullen youth. She always fills his water glass first. He looks away and plays with his hair.

ASH: Looks as though our Leroy's got a little paramour.

LEROY: What did you say?

ASH: A suitor.

LEROY: Jesus Christ, old woman, update your vocabulary.

BEN: One morning, I wake up very early. My head is achy and my chest is tight, so I decide to do some stretching. On my way to the stretching room, I hear sounds coming out of the music room. They don't sound like tambourines or recorders. I peek through a crack in the door. In the corner, tangled up on the floor, Leroy and the brown-haired girl from the restaurant. They have one of those long thin chamois sticks – the kind of thing you put inside clarinets and saxophones to get rid of the moisture – and they're … oh –

LEROY: Are you lost?

BEN: What? No, no.

LEROY: Do you want to use the music room?

BEN: I don't know, maybe.

LEROY: I don't like people looking at me from corners or watching me through cracks. Don't do that.

SCENE NINE

CLARE: As you may have gathered, we have a bit of a 'hands-off' approach to things around here. The Residents are pretty much left to themselves. You never see any doctors or therapists, but you get the sense they're around if you need them.

    The treatment happens at night, after all the Staff has left the Main Complex. There's an alarm – well, not really an alarm, more like a little melody, an escalating series of bells. The doors lock, the air vents click open, and a thin bluish air takes over the rooms and the corridors.

    I'm afraid I can't be any more specific than that. It's not my area. I'm not a scientist or a doctor. I do have basic CPR training, but I've never actually had to use it, knock on wood, so, you know, who knows?

    I'm mainly involved in the hospitality end of things: snacks, activities, trouble-shooting, staffing. I used to work at a spa.

Some of the younger Residents will get a little anxious the first few nights. They'll clutch things, cry, throw their small bodies against the doors, press their small faces against the small glass windows, trying to get out.

I tell them to imagine the treatment like a bunch of small blue furry animals that come out at night to play, crawling around, covering things up with blankets, putting things away in boxes, tidying things up.

I live in a small apartment in the Staff Quarters with my son. It's accessible by an enclosed walkway. We have the basics: a small kitchenette, a computer, a humidifier.

I don't let my son anywhere near the Main Complex.

I would like to say that I had nothing to do with that unfortunate incident with the penguins and that young boy. Those outings were planned independently, and as a mother, I certainly wouldn't recommend traipsing around an icy sea cliff with a bunch of untamed birds.

BEN: It's much more of a workout than you would expect. You can actually get yourself up to a sweat.

CLARE: Yes, you were really flinging that paddle around.

BEN: I had no idea.

CLARE: A dog's never too old to learn new tricks.

BEN: I mean, it just seemed to come out of me: I was moving around, not really thinking, no strategy, and the ball kept getting back over the table somehow.

CLARE: Perhaps by the sheer will of it.

BEN: I guess that's the thing: concentrate on the ball and nothing else.

CLARE: The best way to enjoy a cup of tea is to enjoy the cup of tea, no?

BEN: And there were some of those Japanese children – they were children but were they very good – who actually held their paddles in that professional way, kind of upside down, and I was very surprised to have beaten some of them.

CLARE: Well, fifth place.

BEN: This is really nice, this certificate. This is for me to keep, yes?

CLARE: Yes, you can, you know, do whatever you do with things like that. Put it up on a wall, or –
    My son makes them on the computer. He's handy with … whatever it's called. It keeps him busy. There's not a whole lot for him to do here.

BEN: Well, this is very nice. Tell him I think it's very nice.

CLARE: I'm not very handy with computers. I mean, I can type and open an attachment, but I'm more of a people person.

BEN: Yes, you're very comfortable. I mean, I feel very comfortable around you.

CLARE: Some people click and some people don't. You can't force things.

BEN: No, you wouldn't want to do that.

CLARE: So, otherwise, things are …

BEN: Oh, everything's well. There's the diarrhea and dizziness. I find I'm forgetting simple things, like the names of streets I used to live on, or, um, the names of certain vegetables.
    I find it very dry in here. There's the headaches.
    I often think of my mother and wonder how she's getting on, things like that, you know, things I left behind, my life, and –

CLARE: Well, keep up with the ping-pong.

SCENE TEN

LEROY: Did you see what we're getting for dinner tonight?

ASH: I don't know why you're complaining. You're always complaining.

LEROY: Again, we're getting that sandwich buffet with the sliced meat and the shredded lettuce.

BEN: I don't mind sandwiches for dinner.

LEROY: Well, once in a while, but not twice in one week.

ASH: This is a good place: they have activities and there's often fruit and it's comfortable, so, I mean, you should be grateful you're here and not somewhere else.

BEN: That's what I mean: there are far worse things than sandwiches.

ASH: Someone is obviously paying a lot of money for you to be here, so –

LEROY: They said there would be three full meals a day including a hot dinner, and a sandwich is not a hot dinner, at least not in my country.

BEN: And there's the snacks: the raisins and the corn chips.

ASH: Yes, the corn chips. Thank you, Ben. You see? There are good things here, things to do, things to try, things to involve yourself in. You could make an effort, you know, instead of –

LEROY: I'm just saying, if you start cutting corners in the kitchen, then, I mean, what's next?

ASH: By the way, do you think you could start cleaning your tooth-paste out of the sink? Big globs of it stick to the porcelain and then it hardens and I have to scrape it off with my nail clippers because the cleaning staff seem to be missing it.

LEROY: That's exactly my point.

ASH: What's exactly your point?

LEROY: Sandwich buffets, globs of toothpaste left in the sink: it's a slippery fucking slope.

SCENE ELEVEN

MYA: The sandwich buffet is not as bad as some people make it out to be. It's not just a bunch of kaisers and sliced meat and mustard. I mean, there are kaisers and sliced meat and mustard, but there's more, too. There are tomatoes and olives and cheese and sometimes little pieces of salmon.

I work in food prep and beverage service. When we have the sandwich buffet, it's my job to arrange the meat on the plat-ters and keep the platters full. I have an artistic side, and I was good at sculpture in school.

I'm also responsible for writing the daily menu on a large board outside the restaurant with a thick black marker. My letter-ing is good, and I can write in a straight line without a ruler.

You didn't really have a say in where they sent you. At the Recruitment Centre, they asked you for your top three location choices, but I don't think they took it into consideration too much.

They came to our town and set up a display booth in a mall with information and pictures of exotic locations and how much money you could make. They gave us free doughnuts and juice boxes and lottery tickets.

Most people I knew signed up. Why not? A friend of mine got sent to the Canary Islands, if you can believe it. The lucky bitch. Wherever the hell the Canary Islands are.

CLARE: The Canary Islands are off the coast of Africa.

MYA: We have bimonthly check-ins with the senior staff: performance reviews, mental health check-ins, things like that.

CLARE: Well, your Supervisor has no complaints.

MYA: It's not a complicated job. I don't envy the dishwashers.

CLARE: Some people enjoy washing dishes, and they have those large industrial washers, so ...

MYA: Yeah, I guess, but it can't be fun when we serve the sweet-and-sour chicken. It gets everywhere and it sticks to the plates and I see them having to scrape and scrub them by hand and it gets all over them.

CLARE: The same could be said for the spare ribs, I imagine.

MYA: The spare ribs are popular.

CLARE: Spare ribs are often popular.

MYA: Sometimes I reek like barbecue sauce on my clothes and on my skin and then my room smells like it.

CLARE: Some things can't be helped, working in a kitchen.

MYA: My roommate is teaching me Spanish.

CLARE: You might find you come away with skills you didn't expect you'd learn.

MYA: *Mi nombre es Mya. ¿Quieres acostarte conmigo?*

CLARE: I'm sorry – ?

MYA: I'd be interested in learning some Japanese, but the Japanese workers keep to themselves.

CLARE: In Japan, I've heard, people are reserved; they walk in groups very close together, holding hands. I wouldn't take it personally.

MYA: They're polite, but I think underneath there's something else going on.

CLARE: You've heard about the large blocks of cheese going missing from the kitchen?

MYA: I heard, I guess, but I don't know anything about it.

CLARE: You always have to account for some loss or theft in a kitchen, but the cheese situation is getting out of hand.

MYA: I hope you're not accusing me.

CLARE: No, no, but if you see anything or hear anything –

MYA: I don't.

CLARE: I mean, a block of cheese is not like a chocolate bar, let's say. It would be difficult to smuggle, I would think. Someone would notice something.

MYA: I don't. If I do –

CLARE: That's all I'm asking. It's just something to keep an eye out for.

MYA: I heard people are dying in the Rabbit Wing.

CLARE: What?

MYA: In the kitchen, someone told me.

CLARE: People talk a lot but usually they don't know what they're talking about.

MYA: I heard about eighty or ninety people.

CLARE: Oh, I don't think ninety.

MYA: Yes, but some.

CLARE: Maybe some.

MYA: So how many?

CLARE: Listen, whenever you get large groups of people together there's always things that happen.

MYA: I heard some of them were children.

CLARE: I wouldn't concern yourself with that. I'd focus on your own work.

MYA: I'm not concerned.

CLARE: Just if you were –

MYA: I'm not.

SCENE TWELVE

ASH: I clean up the Observatory. I do some sweeping and dusting. I wash the windows and polish the telescope. I sneak a folding chair out of the music room. A pillow and a blanket. A few sweaters, the blue mittens, the scarf. I drag everything up to the Observatory. Every night, I sit and I watch.

MYA: I'd have a look at the Japanese kids in regards to the cheese situation.

ASH: At first, you think they're all exactly the same, but then you start to notice individual personalities. The way they move, the way they interact, their expressions.

I give them names: Julio and Barbara, Deborah and Baltazar, Tom and Christine, Penelope and Harmony.

They're incredibly social creatures, always doing things in groups, playing little games, climbing on top of each other, building pyramids.

Sometimes they'll gather together in a circle and they'll start dancing, throwing themselves around the ice.

It's funny, it reminds me of the time Jack and Harold and I won this radio contest and got to appear onstage with Johnny Clegg and Savuka, that South African ensemble. They gave us these black-and-white patterned shirts and head wraps to wear and we danced around onstage with the colourful children, banging drums, jumping around like a bunch of –

Or was it Ladysmith Black Mambazo?

SCENE THIRTEEN

BEN: I'm playing ping-pong with my regular partner, a boy named Takashi. He's around thirteen. I'm struggling. I'm completely off my rhythm. I don't feel like myself. I lose the game. Takashi smiles and twirls his paddle in the air. I look at him blankly. 'Why don't you shove that fucking paddle up your ass?'

I don't know where those words come from. I decide to give it a rest for a bit, the ping-pong.

Going back to my room, I pass by some people doing yoga in the stretching room. Maybe I should give that a try.

I lie down on the bed. I keep tossing around. Irritating little itches keep moving around my body, keeping me awake. I don't have any lotion or moisturizer. I suddenly remember Ash's conditioner. I go to the bathroom and take a bottle called Apricot Fusion.

Back in my room, I take off my pyjamas. I spread the conditioner over my skin: my arms, my legs, all my little nooks and crannies. Behind my neck, under my arms, between my legs. My belly. My ass. My penis. My hand. Back and forth. Gently at first, then with more purpose. I try to work something up. Nothing comes.

I look over at the desk. The greeting card. The boy with the violin. His small face, his eyes, watching me. I feel self-conscious. I turn it over, face down on the desk.

I keep at it. Still nothing. Everything feels limp. My head starts to ache.

I give up. I lie down on the bed. Sweaty, sticky, smelling like apricots.

The sound of the ventilation.

ASH: At night, the penguins huddle together. Their shadows creep across the ice. Blue air creeps up the stairwell. I pull a blanket around myself. I wrap the blue scarf around my neck and put the blue mittens on my hands. I lie down on the cold white floor. I feel myself floating on a piece of ice. The penguins surround me, nestling themselves under my arms and between my legs, on my chest, covering me with their thick oily bodies.

The sound of a violin.
A boy appears.

BEN: A sound. Something moving in the corner of the room. The boy on the greeting card, staring at me.

He lifts his violin. He starts to play.
The music. That song.

A woman appears.

I see my mother sitting in a chair beside my bed, her eyes closed, singing quietly.

The boy moves towards me, reaching towards me, his little hands and his little fingers …

SCENE FOURTEEN

LEROY: Little signs and notices start appearing all over the Complex, posted on walls and doors. Things like: 'Regrets will not mend matters.' Or, 'Everything is better with a little artificial sweeten-ing.' Or, 'You can make you own family.'

Sometimes they give you bits of information: 'Cartoon night in the Ostrich Room.' Or, 'Don't block the air vents with wet laundry.'

They say they've been playing around with the ventilation, the treatment, trying a new mix or a new flavour, so if things smell different or feel different it's to be expected.

Whenever I try to get more information or complain, I'm ignored or put off.

In the restaurant, for the second night in a row, some kind of noodle casserole.

CLARE: We encourage criticism, we encourage Residents to contribute to, or participate in –

LEROY: I think the kitchen, there's not a lot of selection lately, and if you consider how much we're paying to be here, I mean, sand-wiches and casseroles aren't really –

CLARE: We want you to be comfortable, so –
What is it exactly that you're saying?

LEROY: I like more meat. I'm European. I'm used to more meat in my diet.

CLARE: There were the spare ribs.

LEROY: Yes, that was last week.

CLARE: And we have the pork chops coming up.

LEROY: Yes, but that's pork, it's not –

CLARE: You can please some people some of the time but you can't please all of the people all of the time.

LEROY: I feel fuzzy, and my head –

CLARE: I think we told you to expect some of that, the treatment –

LEROY: Okay, but is the lack of meat part of the treatment?

CLARE: Well, like I said, you have the pork chops to look forward to.

LEROY: Yes, but pork is not really meat. Pork is –

CLARE: Have you been to the Sunshine Room? Because the Sunshine Room might perk you up.

LEROY: The Sunshine Room is not –
    Yes, I've been to the Sunshine Room, but, I mean, it's not, it's not really sunshine, is it? It's artificial.

CLARE: Of course it's artificial. Everything is artificial.

LEROY: I wrote a letter to my family.

CLARE: You did? That must have been therapeutic.

LEROY: I need you to mail it for me.

CLARE: Correspondence isn't really encouraged.

LEROY: What are you talking about?

CLARE: There are certain controls we need to have, there are certain liberties we need to restrict in order to create an environment that allows us to provide you with the best possible care. I think we were clear from the beginning. Agreements were made, contracts were signed that allow us –

LEROY: I didn't sign anything.

CLARE: Your parents, then.

LEROY: Yes, but if my parents knew –

CLARE: Look, I understand if you're lonely –

LEROY: I'm not lonely.

CLARE: Oh yes, that's right, you've been sneaking around, I've heard, with that girl from the restaurant with the brown hair.

LEROY: So, could you mail this letter for me? Because it's important.

CLARE: No. I can't.

SCENE FIFTEEN

MYA: I just want to say that Leroy isn't always –
I mean, I know he comes off like a bitch, but –
Everyone is scared and lonely. You have to dig deeper than that. You have to look harder.
After we have sex, Leroy kneels over top of me. Naked. His mouth open. I close my eyes.
He draws things in the sweat on my body. My arms, my stomach, my forehead, my thighs, my breasts. Pictures and words.
After, when I'm alone in bed, I can still feel them. The marks he made on my body – his scratches, his indentations, his impressions – on my skin.

SCENE SIXTEEN

LEROY: That night during dinner a group of teenagers sits down at my table. I've never seen them before. They're all wearing tight brown suits and colourful running shoes. They have black hair, thin moustaches and big sunglasses. I think they might be Spanish or Mexican.
They say there are rumours, things are going on, things are happening in other parts of the Complex – the Rabbit Wing, the Billy Goat Wing – and so they're trying to, what did they say, sort things out.

'We see you spending time with that kitchen girl with the brown hair. Maybe you'd like to help us. Maybe you'd like to help us find things out.'

I say, 'What things? Secret recipes?'

They say, 'There are always things to find out, even from a kitchen girl.'

They slide a small piece of paper across the table. They get up and leave.

BEN: Leroy?

LEROY: I put the piece of paper in my pocket.

BEN: Leroy.

LEROY: What?

BEN: Have you seen Ash?

LEROY: No.

BEN: I suppose he's up in the Observatory.

LEROY: I don't know.

BEN: With the penguins.

LEROY: I don't know.

BEN: Are you all right?

LEROY: Yes.

SCENE SEVENTEEN

BEN: I go up to the Observatory. I knock on the door. There's no answer. I go inside. A chair is overturned. Ash is lying on the floor in a small pool of blood. I help him up. I take him down to the bathroom. I clean up the blood and put a cold towel on his head. He's disoriented. He's talking in this kind of panicked, excited whisper.

ASH: At first I thought it was a small animal: a baby seal or a giant squid. The penguins were on top of it, poking at it, and then it started moving, it stood up and I could see –

BEN: It was dark, yes?

ASH: Of course it was dark, it's always dark, but there was light – the moon – and I could see –

BEN: And you fell and banged your head.

ASH: After, yes, I banged my head, but before, that's when I saw him.

BEN: I'm only saying it could have been anything: a shadow, a chunk of ice.

ASH: It wasn't a chunk of ice, it was him.

BEN: And he was …

ASH: He was standing. The penguins were around him, they were petting him –

BEN: Were they aggressive? Did he seem frightened?

ASH: No, he wasn't –
        Look, I know this sounds fantastical.

BEN: I'm just trying to see what you saw.

ASH: Things like this do happen, this is what I'm saying, strange occurrences that are completely unbelievable, but they do happen.

BEN: The thing is, I don't really believe in things like –

ASH: People survive things: kids are found with apes and lions living in caves and under trees, or they get lost at sea and float on a plank for months, or they live in horrible, unlivable conditions, but they survive. So I think it's not impossible the penguins found that young boy and are taking care of him.

BEN: No, you're right, I suppose, it's not completely impossible, but –

ASH: It is possible, Ben.

BEN: I just have a hard time –

ASH: I saw him.

BEN: Well, if you saw him, maybe you should tell someone.

ASH: I'm telling you. (*pause*) Let's keep this to ourselves for now.

BEN: I could be imagining this, but I think Ash might have just made a small pass at me. Did you see that? The way he rested his hand on my forearm, the way he left it there for an inexplicable length of time?

And you know, this isn't the first time I've noticed something from him like an intimate gesture. There was that time in the Observatory when he put his hands on my waist and he leaned in behind me.

I don't know. Male affection isn't something I'm comfortable with.

LEROY: Where's your bitch?

BEN: Excuse me, what did you just say? What did you – ?

LEROY: Your boyfriend.

BEN: Who do you mean? Ash? Who do you mean?

LEROY: I see him looking at you when you're not looking, when you're on the toilet and he's brushing his teeth. I see him looking, sneaking a peak.

BEN: I see you sneaking around with that girl from the restaurant with the brown hair, so I don't know why you're talking to me about secret looks, and besides, maybe what you're seeing is just –

LEROY: What I'm seeing are corners being cut and things not being the way they said they would be and when you ask questions you get put off.

BEN: What are you trying to say?

LEROY: I just think maybe there are things going on here we don't know about or fully understand.

BEN: Well, of course things are going on here we don't know about or fully understand. That's the point.

LEROY: I feel like people are coming into my room at night when I'm asleep and taking things from me. I wake up and things are missing. I forget where I am or how I got here.

BEN: That's normal, you're away from home, you wake up in the night, you're groggy, you're dreaming –

LEROY: I'm not talking about … I'm talking about being lied to and manipulated.

BEN: I don't understand you, Leroy, I don't understand people like you who have to punch their way through life, who have to pick at things and question things and look for problems in things, because I don't know how you can live like that.

LEROY: It's not just me, other people are talking, other people are –

BEN: Sometimes you just have to trust that other people know what's best for you, because how can you have perspective or your own life. You can't, you can't see it.

LEROY: Maybe you're the one who can't see. You can't see or you don't want to see.

BEN: Look, why don't you go play with your little friend from the kitchen, because if you've got nothing to contribute –

LEROY: Why don't you go fuck yourself.

BEN: Excuse me, Mister. If you've got nothing to contribute to this conversation except paranoia and gossip …

CLARE: I think it's important to understand this is hard for everyone.

Sometimes I'll be sitting in a chair and I'll be watching my child sleep, or I'll be watching ice move outside the window, and I'll think about my home, and I can't remember what cupboard the salad bowl is in or what colour the bathroom rug is or if my sister wears earrings, so it's not just –

Memories, you know, they're like children. You make them, you care for them, you live with them, they leave you. You try to hang onto them – there they go, running away from you. Anyway.

What do they say?

'Loss is necessary. You have to bleed the wound, clean out the poison, before you can really address the injury.'

SCENE EIGHTEEN

BEN: You can barely find any room to sit in the restaurant now. Everyone is squished together. Some people have to eat standing up. I've heard rumours they're thinking about doing away with table service altogether and setting up a permanent buffet.

CLARE: I really don't think that's going to happen.

BEN: Tonight it's Wing Night. There are bowls of dipping sauces on the table: honey garlic, sweet and sour, barbecue.

Ash has started taking his meals up in the Observatory, so I've been eating alone lately. Every night, he fills his pockets with food and sneaks off. And you know, I don't want to be critical, but I don't think it's healthy, spending all that time up there alone.

ASH: At first they were tentative, looking away, being coy. Like any new relationship, there were problems, arguments, adjustments. But now, they're inseparable. Tender and devoted and loving.

The penguins feed him small pieces of fish, they take him on their backs and slide across the ice. They cover him, rubbing his body with their oily skin, protecting him from the wind and the cold.

The boy teaches them new games to play: leapfrog, Simon Says, Red Rover. He tells them stories and draws pictures in the snow. At night he sings to them, sweet little lullabies.

I clap along, singing quietly to myself up in the Observatory, gnawing on a pocketful of cold sticky chicken wings.

BEN: Anyway, I'm about to give the honey garlic a try. A man comes up behind me and puts his hands on my shoulders. He starts shaking me and kisses the top of my head. We had apparently taught together at a music conservatory years ago. He's an oboist and he used to live in my old neighbourhood.

'Remember the children in their uniforms? The red jackets and the red ties? The red plastic chairs? The afternoon recitals under the trees?'

I look up at him. Honey garlic sauce is all over my hands and all over the table. I don't know what to say. I've never seen him before in my life.

He pulls a chair over, he leans into me and he starts talking about some horrible things that are going on.

He says it's not safe anymore. People are going missing all the time. There are uniformed patrols rounding people up: addicts, or people who look like addicts, or people who might look like addicts. There are apparently rewards being offered, financial compensations, if you bring these addicts in to these … um … warehouses, I think he called them. He doesn't know who runs them.

If you don't have any money or don't know the right people, they'll apparently ship you off to a cut-rate Recovery Centre, one of the experimental ones.

He said there are rumours of an island off the coast of Croatia where they bleed you on a regular basis and hook you up to machines. Apparently, there's a place in Florida where they inject you with chemicals and use restraints. They stack you up one on top of another, they put you in compartments like chickens at a chicken farm and they do things to you.

He leans in closer. He grabs my arm. He digs his nails into my skin.

I start to feel a little uncomfortable, a little gassy, from the chicken wings maybe, or maybe from the oboist. I'm not sure. I excuse myself and go back to my room.

SCENE NINETEEN

LEROY: Are you sure it's safe?

MYA: I told you, my roommate's working nights in the bakery now, so …

LEROY: It smells funny.

MYA: When you work in a kitchen, smells follow you.

LEROY: I wouldn't want to do your job. How much do you get paid?

MYA: They deposit it directly into my account, so I'm not exactly sure.

LEROY: I just think someone must be making a load of money here. When you think of how much we pay and there's so many of us, if you add it up, someone is making a fucking load.

MYA: There are more coming every week.

LEROY: Where are they putting them all?

MYA: Some of the new Residents have to share a room.

LEROY: What do you mean?

MYA: In the Panda Wing, I heard there are four to a room. Everyone sleeps together and you get a small locker for your things.

LEROY: That's disgusting.

MYA: Anyway, I've heard things are a bit out of control in the Panda Wing.

LEROY: It's bad enough sharing a bathroom, but if I had to sleep with strangers in my room –

MYA: I shared a room with a brother and two sisters until I was sixteen.

LEROY: Watching me, breathing at me.

MYA: I got used to having people around me.

LEROY: Well, I would hate that. I would complain.

MYA: You would complain. There's something new.

LEROY: Maybe if more people complained there would be less things to complain about.

MYA: Tell me something.

LEROY: What?

MYA: Something intimate, something personal.

LEROY: What do you mean?

MYA: Tell me what your favourite book is. Tell me about a vacation you took. A favourite song. A nickname. Your first crush. A game you used to play. A toy. A pet.

LEROY: A pet?

MYA: Anything. Something.

LEROY: I'm sorry, I just think maybe there are more important things to talk about.

Pause.

MYA: I should have a shower because it can't be nice for you, me standing here smelling like deep-fried chicken wings.

LEROY: Mya takes her clothes off. She walks into the bathroom and turns on the shower. Steam fills up the room. I take a crumpled piece of paper out of my pocket: 'Midnight. The Coyote Wing. Room 324.'

MYA: My Mom used to say, 'Mya, you shoulda been born in a different time. Looking for romance, you're gonna be disappointed. Romance is finished. The world's a different place. Look around.' I put my head out of the shower. Leroy's gone.

SCENE TWENTY

BEN: Back in my room, practising yoga. I'm standing on one leg, my other leg pressed against my thigh, my arms raised up. I have trouble focusing. I keep thinking about that strange oboist and the disturbing things he was saying.

The children. The red jackets. The red ties. The red chars.

I feel a sharp pain behind my eyes and in my mouth. A spasm goes through my body. I start to shake. My muscles seize up. My legs give out. I fall forward. I black out.

A boy appears.
The sound of a violin.

Something on top of me, nudging me awake. A shadow. A face. The boy. The violin. That song. The music pulls me up. It pulls me out of the room. I'm walking down a long white corridor. The corridor is made of ice: the walls, the floor, the ceiling, all ice. At the end of the corridor, in the ice, a tiny picture, hazy and smudged. A woman on a chair, a small boy in bed beside her. She's singing to him and –

CLARE: Oh. Hi.

BEN: Hi. Um. I'm sorry.

CLARE: What are you doing here?

BEN: I was walking, and I guess I got turned around.

CLARE: You're not supposed to be here.

BEN: I don't know how I got here.

CLARE: You shouldn't be here.

BEN: No, I didn't mean to –

CLARE: I thought I heard something and I was frightened.

BEN: No, I wouldn't want people knocking around outside my door at night peeking in my windows.

CLARE: Are you all right?

BEN: Oh, no no no, I'm fine.

CLARE: My son is asleep, so –

BEN: No, I didn't mean to disturb you.

CLARE: I thought I heard someone.

BEN: I got completely turned around: my mind was wandering and, apparently, so were my feet.

CLARE: Are you sure you're – ?

BEN: No, no, I'm – (*pause*) How's your son?

CLARE: Well, he's asleep, he's fine. (*pause*) How's the ping-pong?

BEN: The ping-pong isn't really working out anymore.

CLARE: Oh, that's too bad.

BEN: Well, I've been taking some of those yoga classes instead.

CLARE: I think it's good you're taking advantage of the activities.

BEN: I think the yoga might be good for me because –

CLARE: Yoga is good for the mind and for the body.

BEN: How's your son?

CLARE: He's fine. I told you. He's asleep.

BEN: It must be hard for him.

CLARE: My son?

BEN: All cooped up, nothing to do, no one to play with.

CLARE: Well, he has me. We have each other.

BEN: I was just thinking, maybe I could come by and spend some time with him.

CLARE: I'm sorry?

BEN: You know, talk, play a game, go for a walk, teach him something, an instrument, or –

CLARE: Oh, like a Big Brother?

BEN: Yes.

CLARE: Well, that's kind of you.

BEN: Like a Big Brother.

CLARE: But, you know, no.

BEN: I was just thinking, maybe you've got a little Vivaldi there.

CLARE: He doesn't really show an interest in music.

BEN: I was just thinking –

CLARE: Do you need help back to your room? Because I could call someone.

BEN: Back in my room. The card is lying open on the desk.
    'Loss is necessary.' I hear those words in my head.
    I pick up the card. I gently tear it into pieces. I go to the bathroom and flush it down the toilet.
    The boy, the music, swirl around the toilet bowl. Pieces of his face stick to the porcelain. Pieces of his arm, his chest, his hands, his mouth. I have to flush three times before he's completely gone.

I go back to my room. I take my clothes off. I stand under the air vent, naked, my head up, my mouth open.

The sound of the ventilation.
Shadows appear.

SCENE TWENTY-TWO

ASH: I see them coming across the ice. Large shadows, moving slowly. Machines. Large metal claws and long piercing drills. They start boring holes into the ice.

Rows of children dressed in white parkas and face coverings are dragging large heavy sacks across the ice and dropping them into the holes. The sacks are set on fire. Flames shoot up. Heavy smoke spreads out across the ice.

The penguins are stumbling around confused and disoriented, shielding their faces from the heat and the smoke, some of them sprawled out on the ice, rolling back and forth, gasping, vomiting.

The boy gathers them together. He starts leading them away. The boy out in front, the penguins behind him. Dragging themselves across the ice. Looking for sanctuary.

LEROY: What are you doing here?

ASH: It seems there's some shuffling going on.

LEROY: What?

ASH: There's a Spanish couple who've moved into my room and I have this piece of paper that says I'm to move in here. It appears we're being squeezed together.

126 | GREG MACARTHUR

PART TWO

SCENE ONE

Ben, Ash and Leroy are all wearing identical brown outfits.

BEN: Well, you have to laugh. Putting Ash in with Leroy, it's like putting the monkeys in with the lions. Anyway, they shouldn't complain. Two to a room is nothing. An Egyptian family has moved into my room. There are seven of them. The younger children have taken over my bed so I'm sleeping on the floor now. They've given me a small inflatable mattress. I sleep in the corner under the air vent.

There've been a few other minor adjustments. There are new buffet tables in the restaurant. Everything's plastic now: the tables, the trays, the cutlery, the plates. Everyone lines up one behind the other. It's good to get there early, as they often run out of food and –

Um –

They've turned the sunshine off in the Sunshine Room. There was some kind of leak, there was screaming, I don't know the details.

There's no more ping-pong. Balls were continually being lost or broken and, due to budgetary restraints, they stopped ordering more. There's still the yoga, though. Those yoga people are … what's the word … resilient.

We're responsible for cleaning our own rooms now. They've installed a series of long metal shafts throughout the Complex. Dirty linen, garbage, it's all thrown down the shafts, taken out across the ice to one of the new incinerating stations and burned.

They've given us these new outfits to wear. There was an outbreak or a breakout or something. Something spread, people got sick. Apparently fabric was involved.

They collected all of our contaminated clothing and gave us these. There was a choice between light brown and dark brown. Some people took a light brown top and a dark brown pant, or vice versa, to mix things up.

Some of the younger Residents have taken to rolling up the

pant legs or doing something with the collar, but I don't know about that. They're itchy and bunch up at the crotch. But, you know, you can get used to anything over time.

There are twelve of us sharing the bathroom now. It takes more planning and scheduling, but I think we've worked out a good system.

ASH: The Spanish couple take their bath together at night, the Egyptians in the morning, me and Ben in the afternoon –

BEN: Not together.

ASH: And Leroy squeezes in wherever he can. He hides in his bed, under his blankets, scribbling into a small leather notebook. He sleeps with his face buried in his pillow.

LEROY: Can you not talk about me, please? Can you maybe talk about something else?

SCENE TWO

CLARE: I think it will be only temporary.

ASH: It's fine.

CLARE: It wasn't up to me. There are other people who make these decisions.

ASH: Of course there are.

CLARE: We're all doing what we can to make everyone as comfortable as possible under the circumstances.

ASH: No, I think everything's fine, everything's –

CLARE: Well, you know what they say.

ASH: What's that?

CLARE: Life is a series of adjustments.

ASH: Is that what they say?

CLARE: Anyway, I hear you've been spending a lot of time up in the Observatory.

ASH: Yes, um –

CLARE: One of the cleaners heard something –

ASH: Is it a problem?

CLARE: You're not really supposed to be up there.

ASH: I'm sorry, I didn't realize –

CLARE: What are you doing up there?

ASH: Well, there's that telescope, and –

CLARE: You like geography or astronomy or –

ASH: Actually, no, it's the penguins.

CLARE: The penguins?

ASH: I enjoy watching the penguins.

CLARE: Well, as long as I don't start to hear about any, you know, wild orgy parties or –

ASH: No, no, just me and the penguins.

CLARE: And everything else is –

ASH: Yes, everything else is –

CLARE: Okey-dokey.

ASH: Actually, there is something.

CLARE: Mm hm?

ASH: Those incinerators they're building out on the ice.

CLARE: I'm sorry?

ASH: It's just … I'm worried about the penguins.

CLARE: The penguins?

ASH: I'm worried about what's going to happen to the penguins because –

CLARE: Yes, you know, I would perhaps spend less time worrying about the penguins and more time worrying about yourself.

ASH: I'm just worried that –

CLARE: I mean, I don't know, maybe it's just me, but if I see something that worries me or upsets me, I usually look the other way.

ASH: No, no, of course, I was just –

CLARE: Perhaps the thing to do is to stay away from the Observatory, to stop playing around with the telescope, to stop looking at things that aren't really your concern, because we don't want people looking at things and getting upset.

ASH: No, you're right, I shouldn't be –

CLARE: Don't get me wrong, I think it's good you're taking an interest in things, because we want everyone to enjoy themselves, and, you know, there are some Residents who just don't seem to be enjoying themselves at all, or seem to make a conscious effort not to enjoy themselves.

ASH: Yes, I heard about that scuffle in the Panda Wing.

CLARE: Scuffle?

ASH: The cleaners who were taken hostage by those Venezuelans.

CLARE: I don't know where you get your information from. All this gossip, it's like a schoolyard in here. Anyway, they weren't Venezuelans, so –

ASH: Mya was telling me. She said –

CLARE: Okay then.

LEROY: What a condescending fucking bitch.

SCENE THREE

MYA: The Venezuelan incident put everyone on edge.

CLARE: They weren't Venezuelans. I don't know why people keep saying that.

MYA: Increased security measures are put in place. Everyone is being monitored more closely. There are new safety buzzers in the corridors. There are new security locks on all the doors. The Panda Wing is quarantined.

CLARE: Temporarily, just temporarily.

MYA: 'Any unauthorized interaction between Staff and Residents is strictly prohibited.'
     Me and Leroy have to be more careful. He's been secretive and paranoid. I mean, more secretive and paranoid. He's always

sitting in corners, watching things, writing in a small leather notebook.

He's been hanging out with these new friends. I think they're Mexican or Spanish or something. He's always sneaking off at night to meet with them.

LEROY: They call themselves the Terminators.

MYA: The Terminators?

LEROY: We're gathering information. That's all I can tell you. There's other underground groups or cells operating in different parts of the Complex.

MYA: He won't eat in the restaurant anymore. I sneak him food when I can.

LEROY: They say, 'Be careful who you talk to and be more careful who you listen to. The corridors have ears.'

MYA: I've been promoted to Breakfast Shift Supervisor.

LEROY: What does that mean?

MYA: I do the scheduling and the inventory and I get a raise, but I have to get up at 4:30 in the morning, so –

LEROY: Did you hear about the family that tried to escape?

MYA: No. What?

LEROY: There were four of them. They crawled out through a ventilation duct in the Billy Goat Wing. Their bodies were found sprawled out on the ice.

MYA: I didn't hear anything about that.

LEROY: Someone said they were shot.

MYA: I don't think so.

LEROY: And they have dogs now.

MYA: What?

LEROY: They have guard dogs patrolling outside.

MYA: I think maybe those new friends of yours are putting things in your head.

LEROY: 'If you think it's true it probably is.'

MYA: I'll ask around. I'll see what I can find out.

Mya gives Leroy a plastic container.

MYA: Here.

LEROY: What is this?

MYA: Some kind of fish stew.

LEROY: What's in it?

MYA: Fish. Or some kind of fish product.

LEROY: What's fish product?

MYA: I don't know. There's not a lot of selection in the kitchen anymore. I'm doing what I can.

Leroy gives the container back to Mya.

LEROY: They want to meet you.

MYA: Who?

LEROY: The Terminators.

MYA: 'Paranoia is the most addictive drug of them all.' On the way back to my room, I see those words scribbled on the wall in thick black letters.

SCENE FOUR

BEN: I go to the stretching room for our Wednesday night yoga class but the stretching room is closed. There's a notice posted on the door: 'All extracurricular activities have been suspended. Residents are discouraged from participating in any unsupervised, non-sanctioned group activities.'

We all stand around, not sure what to do. A few people spread out and do some exercises right there in the corridor, as some kind of protest. The floor is sticky and cold and smells like urine. Everyone gives up.

I go back to my room. One of the Egyptian kids has vomited all over my inflatable mattress. A pasty clump. I take off one of my socks and rub at it but it just spreads it around and now my sock is dirty.

I turn the mattress over. I lie down. I put the dirty sock back on my foot. I stare up into the air vent. It's still a few hours until ventilation. I stand on a chair. I press my face against the vent. I lick the vent with my tongue, trying to get some of the residue off the grate.

SCENE FIVE

CLARE: I'm sorry to interrupt, but we have a little, well a big, actually, a big and exciting announcement to make that concerns everyone, so –

Feedback.

Whoops. Okey-dokey. I won't keep everyone in suspense. We're going to be building a new Complex.

Feedback.

And this new Complex, it's going to be much larger: we're going to be able to almost triple our capacity. That's going to make everyone happy, it's going to be very state-of-the-art and it's, well, its going to be eye-catching: lots of metal and steel, and lots of metal. And there are going to be some exciting additions: a small amphitheatre, research facilities, a gymnasium, a gift centre, an enclosed play area with a small ride. It's going to be a major undertaking, but in the end —

BEN: And then she says something about some kind of Work Reward Program.

CLARE: The Work Reward Program is exciting and innovative and we're very excited about it.

BEN: There are things like bonuses or points you can earn towards, um, your debt load, or certain privileges or access to something. I don't know, I don't understand it exactly, it's a complicated system, but it's all explained in the package.

CLARE: You've all been assigned activities, and if you don't like the activities you've been assigned, you can request another activity be assigned to you. Every request will be considered, but please keep in mind a consideration does not mean an accommodation.

ASH: I don't understand. What did she just say?

LEROY: What is this? Work assignments –

CLARE: We prefer to think of them as life activities, not work –

LEROY: This is fucking unbelievable.

CLARE: Helping you to help yourself. There are a million and one things to be done, so no one is going to be left out. There's going to be something for everyone.

BEN: What did you … ?

ASH: Hm?

BEN: What did you get?

ASH: Interior design. Wooden fixtures. You?

BEN: An orchestra. A children's orchestra.

LEROY: I tear up my activity sheet. I go look for the Terminators.

SCENE SIX

CLARE: Are you enjoying your new position?

MYA: I don't like getting up early.

CLARE: Nobody does, but somebody has to.

MYA: Also, the chafing dishes aren't being cleaned properly at night, so when we come in in the mornings we have to scrub everything down again and we get behind.

CLARE: I'll talk to the night staff.

MYA: They're also not emptying the garbage.

CLARE: Is there anything else?

MYA: I heard they have dogs.

CLARE: What?

MYA: Someone told me they have guard dogs outside the Complex.

CLARE: Well, I wouldn't know about that.

MYA: And guns.

CLARE: Who told you that?

MYA: Someone.

CLARE: Someone ... ?

MYA: I hear things.

CLARE: Yes, I know what you mean, I hear things too. I hear you're still sneaking around with that Dutch boy.

MYA: What?

CLARE: Sneaking food out of the kitchen. Sneaking into his room after work.

MYA: Who told you that?

CLARE: People see things. People talk about things. You're not the only one around here with eyes, ears and a mouth.

MYA: Well –

CLARE: 'Any unauthorized interaction between Staff and Residents is strictly prohibited.'

MYA: I know that, but –

CLARE: I've been looking the other way because I like you, but I think now you'd do better to start keeping a professional distance.

MYA: He won't eat in the restaurant anymore, so maybe sometimes I bring him some leftovers, but –

CLARE: Look, I'm not saying you can't be kind, but in the end, the appearance of caring and actually caring usually have the same effect, so –

Things are happening. You should start looking out for yourself. You don't want to be left behind.

MYA: What are you saying?

CLARE: You have, what, another year left on your contract? And then you can go where you like and you can do what you like with whoever you like. But for now, it's probably best if you don't cause any problems.

MYA: That night after work I sneak back into the kitchen. I take some food out of the food lockup and put it in my knapsack. I pull my sweater over my face. I walk down the corridor. The Coyote Wing. Room 324. The Terminators.

People are sitting on the floor. White cloths tied over their faces. Old bed sheets, eye holes sliced out, tied with string and shoelaces.

The air vent is covered in plastic. The plastic makes a strange flapping sound. Everyone looks at me.

I take the food out of my knapsack and put it in the centre of the room. I sit down beside Leroy. He ties a white cloth over my face. He puts his hand on the back of my neck. My whole body goes limp.

SCENE SEVEN

BEN: The orchestra practices in a small room beside one of the incinerating shafts. It's hot but well-lit. The children sit in rows of chairs in front of me. They're grey and thin. Their mouths hang open.

I tell them to pick up an instrument. They don't move. They stare at me blankly. I tell them, 'Look. This will be good for you. This will help you. We all have to make a contribution. We all have to do something. Would you rather be outside hauling metal or digging holes?'

I raise my voice. I raise my arms. They raise their instruments.

The children's orchestra is heard.

We practice day and night. The children's lips blister, they crack and bleed. Drops of blood all over the instruments and all over the floor. Their bodies heave, every note, every breath, a punch in the chest. I tell them, 'Nothing comes without a little sacrifice.'

I lose some of them. Their bodies give out. They fall off their chairs onto the floor.

I call Security. Two men come by wearing thick gloves and face coverings. They stuff the bodies into sacks. Sometimes two or three to a sack. They drag them away. I look at the empty chairs.

They say, 'Don't worry. We'll bring you replacements. There's no lack of children around here.'

Instruments, on the other hand –

We don't have a lot and the ones we have are not in good shape. At night, after practice, I clean them with a thick white cloth. The children's saliva, their blood, I wipe it all away. I keep the instruments in a small closet beside the music room for safe-keeping.

They start broadcasting our rehearsals throughout the Complex. Day and night, music fills up the corridors. The beautiful sound of sacrifice and obedience, the sound of harmony, the sound of people working together.

SCENE EIGHT

ASH: Two men come up to the Observatory with large hammers, screw guns and blowtorches. They rip the telescope apart. They smash the large glass lens. They leave everything in pieces all over the floor.

They bring in some carving tools, buckets of varnish and blocks of wood.

I start making wooden doorknobs. I have a quota of fifteen doorknobs a day. Every few days, two men come by to collect them. Sometimes they bring me food. I never leave the Observatory. I work fifteen, sixteen hours a day. My hands become blistered and swollen. I soak them in a bucket of varnish. They burn for a few minutes and then I feel nothing.

At night I sit in front of the window, my hands covered in varnish, looking out at the ice.

I can't see anything.

I hear voices. Small, broken, crawling across the ice, through the dark, towards me. The voices press against the glass. The glass starts to crack, the voices seep in, they fill up the Observatory, swirling around me, pulling at me –

Glass shatters.
A boy appears.

SCENE NINE

CLARE: My son has gone missing.

I came home from work. The door was open. The computer was on. His shoes were beside the door.

They say, 'It's not your fault. These things happen. He might have gotten outside, fallen into the water, a hole in the ice, an incinerator. One of the Residents might have … There are a thousand possibilities. It's best not to think about it. Go back to your room. We'll do what we can.'

They put up posters. They interview Residents and Staff. They use dogs and helicopters. They give me a two-week paid leave of absence. Where am I going to go?

I lie in his bed and I bury myself in his dirty clothes. I put his small white T-shirt over my face.

I walk through the Complex – the Rabbit Wing, the Swan Wing, the Woodpecker Wing, the Billy Goat Wing – looking through rooms, in piles of garbage, down incinerator shafts, at the faces of Residents.

Music follows me down corridors. Children playing instruments.

In a small storage closet beside the music room, I stand in the dark and I listen. Instruments vibrate on shelves around me.

SCENE TEN

BEN: Clare?

CLARE: I enjoyed that.

BEN: What are you doing in here?

CLARE: What was that?

BEN: I'm sorry?

CLARE: The music your children were playing. What was it? Vivaldi?

BEN: What? No.

CLARE: Because I remember you telling me you wanted my child. You wanted to teach him Vivaldi.

BEN: I don't – What?

CLARE: It wasn't Vivaldi?

BEN: No.

CLARE: My son's gone missing.

BEN: Your son?

CLARE: I thought maybe you knew something.

BEN: No, why would I – ?

CLARE: You seem to be fond of children.

BEN: I don't know anything.

CLARE: You don't know anything.

BEN: No.

CLARE: No.

BEN: Are you – Can I call someone?

CLARE: You don't know anything.

BEN: No. I told you. (*pause*) Anyway. What do they say? 'Loss is necessary. You have to bleed the wound –

CLARE: What did you say?

BEN: You shouldn't be in here. It's not safe. Clare –

CLARE: What did you – ?

BEN: I call Security. They drag Clare out of the closet. She grabs a wooden tambourine off the shelf and smashes it on the floor. It breaks into pieces. It's the only tambourine we have.

SCENE ELEVEN

CLARE: They take me to a room with a small window, a steel basin and a toilet. I've never been in this room before. They put me in a plastic chair.

Two men come into the room. One man gives me a glass of water. The other man says, 'Clare, we like you. You're a valuable member of this facility. But we can't have you sneaking around, interfering with Residents, asking questions, taking things into your own hands. It's not safe.'

The man who gave me the glass of water leaves the room. The other man continues talking.

'We're going to help you through this difficult time.'

I finish my glass of water but I don't know what to do with the empty glass and so I put it beside my chair. I suddenly worry that I might knock the glass over with my feet and so I put the glass directly under my chair.

The man crouches down in front of my face.

'Good things are happening here and you're a part of them. Of course, we had some problems with the Rabbits and the Pandas early on but we learned from that. The Swans are completely non-sexual. The Billy Goats and the Coyotes are becoming more and more trusting. The Salamanders and the Woodpeckers remember only what we want them to remember. We're making progress with fear and appetite and instinct. Children and old people are still giving us some problems, but you know children and old people. They fall apart at the drop of a hat.'

The man smiles and squeezes my shoulders. 'You're a strong healthy woman so I wouldn't worry.'

He reaches down and picks up the glass from under my chair. He leaves the room. The door locks. There's a clicking sound. Large air vents open all around me. I turn my head. Outside the small window, I see something moving out on the ice.

SCENE TWELVE

ASH: I cover myself in varnish: my arms, my legs, my chest, my face. I wrap myself in blankets. A pair of old blue mittens, an old blue scarf, I wrap it around my head and my face.

Out of the Observatory. Out on the ice. The cold air sticks to me. I start walking.

My feet are heavy in the snow. The air is thick and black. The ice is black. Everything exposed and rotten.

The boy is in front of me. His face is red and scabby. Most of his teeth are gone and his lips are black. His skin is oily and blistered.

He's surrounded by bodies. Hundreds of bodies. Their lifeless flesh, their blank expressions, spilled all over the ice. I can't tell them apart. They all look exactly the same. Their idiosyncrasies, their personalities, gone. They're nothing.

Impressions, imitations, remnants of life.

The boy looks up at me. He's shivering. Small tears are frozen onto his face.

I put the blue mittens on his small hands. I wrap the blue scarf around his small neck. He walks away from me, towards the edge of the water. The blue scarf catches a bit of wind and flies up.

And then he's gone.

SCENE THIRTEEN

LEROY: Did you notice there were only twelve of us tonight?

MYA: The Portuguese couple wasn't there.

LEROY: The Portuguese couple has been missing for two days.

MYA: And the Russians.

LEROY: They come to your room at night and they take you away. We have to be more careful. The corridors have eyes.

MYA: I think my roommate is spying on me. The way she looks at me. I don't know.

LEROY: You can't trust anybody. Keep your eyes open.

MYA: Every night we meet up in the Terminator's room. I bring food and other supplies. Whatever they ask for: black markers, kitchen knives, security codes, old tablecloths. We discuss things, we exchange information. Things we hear, things we see, things that are happening. Everything is written down. The Terminators tell us to keep a record of everything.

LEROY: 'People believe what they read. Write something down, it's true. Give something words, it lives.'

MYA: There are lies everywhere. Everything is poisonous. Believe everything. Believe nothing. I don't know. I'm not a political person. I don't see things that way.

I see Leroy.

I guess everyone believes what they have to believe. Everyone sees what they have to see to get by.

LEROY: We tie white cloths over our faces. We spread out across the Complex. We tear down their posters. We scratch out their words.

We write our own.

MYA: I hand Leroy a thick black marker. He stands on a chair. He reaches up. I put my hands around his waist. I press my face against his back. On the wall in front of him he writes in thick black letters, (*the phrase is projected on a screen*) 'Silent weapons, quiet wars.'

SCENE FOURTEEN

BEN: I go up the stairs to the Observatory. I knock on the door. There's no answer. I creep inside. The floor is covered in sawdust, scraps of clothes, food, broken glass, excrement. Ash is sitting on the floor. He's holding a piece of wood. All around him, in the sawdust, on the window ledges, on the floor, these small wooden –

Many small wooden penguins appear.

ASH: Who is it?

BEN: It's Ben.

ASH: Ben.

BEN: It's been a while. I've been meaning to visit, but, you know, you get caught up in things.

ASH: Yes.

BEN: I'm sorry but – What are all these?

ASH: They're penguins.

BEN: Penguins?

ASH: Wooden penguins.

BEN: Jesus, there must be –

ASH: Almost a hundred.

BEN: You've been busy.

ASH: And you.

BEN: I'm sorry?

ASH: I hear you. Your children. Your music.

BEN: Oh, well –

ASH: Creeping around corridors, up stairwells like ghosts.

BEN: I think they're coming along. They brought me a Korean girl a while ago who actually had her own violin. Unfortunately, she died after a couple of weeks. But we have a violin now, so –

ASH: Ben is standing in the shadow of the doorway. I can barely see him. He looks far away. He's holding something in his hand. He moves across the room and presses his face against the window.

BEN: God, it's really something, isn't it?

ASH: I'm sorry?

BEN: The new Complex.

ASH: Yes.

BEN: I didn't realize how large it's going to be. Look at it, spreading out across the ice like a –

ASH: Like a plague, wiping everything away.

BEN: I'm disappointed to hear you say that. I mean, you hear this kind of paranoid negative talk from some people, but you don't expect to hear it from your friends. (*pause*) Look at all they've done for us. Look at it. And you, sitting up here, being critical, being judgmental, being resentful. You might try to show a bit of appreciation. A bit of enthusiasm. Tidy up a bit. Clean yourself up a bit. They're not taking everyone. Some people are going to be left behind, and I don't think –

ASH: Did you want something?

BEN: Oh. Yes. Um. This tambourine, it got a little battered up. It's the only one we have, so –
    I thought you might be able to fix it.

ASH: I don't think there's anything I can do for you.

BEN: I just thought with your tools and wood, you might be able to –

ASH: There's nothing I can do.

BEN: Well –

ASH: If you could close the door when you leave.

BEN: On my way out, I accidentally trip over one of the penguin figurines. Its head breaks off and rolls across the floor.

SCENE FIFTEEN

MYA: It's late. I'm getting ready to go meet Leroy. Two men come into my room. They have guns. They shine a light on my face. 'Come with us. Now.'

My roommate sits up in bed and smiles.

They take me outside and put me in a small vehicle. They drive me across the ice, past the incinerators and the fires. Dogs chase after us.

They take me into the new Complex. Doors lock behind us. They take me up an elevator and into a dark room. I see large white buckets, loose electrical wiring, long metal tables. They turn on fluorescent lights. Everything vibrates and hums. It takes a few seconds for my eyes to adjust.

The men smile. They start clapping. 'Congratulations,' they say.

I've been made Head Supervisor of Kitchen #7.

They take me to my new room, a single room with a window.

I stand in front of the window over the heating vent. The window is wet, dripping with condensation. The old Complex is blurry and far away.

They say, 'Make yourself comfortable. Someone will pack up your things and bring them over. You won't be going back there. There's a lot of work to do. Get some sleep. It's going to be a busy few weeks.'

I write a word on the window with my finger.

A word appears on the screen.

SCENE SIXTEEN

LEROY: I wait for Mya outside the restaurant. I wait for almost an hour. She doesn't show up. I go to the Terminators' room. They're gone. The room is empty and smells like disinfectant.

Two men are in the room. One man is mopping the floor. The other man is holding a file folder. The man with the file folder says, 'It's come to our attention that you're not pulling your weight and, well, it's time for you to start pulling your weight.'

The man with the file folder taps the file folder with his finger.

'You have to do something, because there are consequences if you don't. We can send you away. We can trade you, sell you to a Centre in, say, I don't know, Florida. And we don't think you'd want to end up in Florida. We have the authority to do that. We can do that. And other things.'

The man who's mopping stops mopping.

'You don't have to see this as a problem. You can see this as an opportunity. It's better than being out there, in the world.'

He tells me to report to the Elephant Room tomorrow at 7 a.m. I'm going to be working outside on a scaffold installing metal panels.

They take me back to my room.

Nothing stays with you. You try to hang onto things. Everything goes away.

The sound of the ventilation.

I take my clothes off. I lie down on the bed. I feel Mya's hands on me. Her fingers on my skin. Words on my body.

On the floor beside my bed, a white cloth and a brown leather notebook. I leave the white cloth on the floor. I pick up the notebook. I tilt my head back. I open my eyes and my mouth.

SCENE SEVENTEEN

BEN: The Big Shuffle. The Opening of the New Complex. The Relocation. We're all being moved over together. Marched across the ice. One giant migration. The Rabbits, the Coyotes, the Billy Goats, the Swans, the Crocodiles, the Pandas, the Woodpeckers. They've given us these new animal buttons to wear so we don't get all mixed up, and I think they're really impressive: the colour, the shape, the handicraft.

A real mark of distinction. A symbol of allegiance. A badge of honour.

I'm proud to be a Woodpecker. I'm proud and hopeful. I'm looking forward. What do they say? 'There's no sense looking back over your shoulder. There's nothing there. Whatever was there is gone. Everything you need is right here.'

CLARE: Ben.

BEN: Jesus. Clare?

CLARE: Hi.

BEN: Hi. Clare –

CLARE: Is everything all right?

BEN: Yes. No. I'm sorry. It's just –
I didn't expect to see you again. I thought you –
But here you are.

CLARE: Here I am.

BEN: Yes.

CLARE: Anyway, listen, we were wondering if your children's orchestra would like to perform a little something at the Opening Ceremonies?

BEN: Well, wow.

CLARE: We're putting together the program and we thought –

BEN: That would be an honour.

CLARE: People like children. People like watching children do things.

BEN: I think the kids will be excited.

CLARE: We thought maybe you could write something special, an original composition.

BEN: Oh –

CLARE: Something snappy and upbeat, something memorable, something you can clap along to.

BEN: Of course.

CLARE: Okay then.

BEN: Did they ever find your – ?

CLARE: Sorry?

BEN: Your –

CLARE: My ... hm?

BEN: Um ...

CLARE: We're a bit under the gun, so the sooner you can get to it.

BEN: I head back to my room. I walk slowly through the corridors, humming to myself. I'm looking for something inside my head: a song, a melody, something inspirational, something memorable, something –

The sound of a violin.

Something ...um ...

A woman appears.

At the end of a long corridor, lying on the floor, I see an old woman crumpled up in ball. She's completely naked except for a ... what do you call it? A ...

CLARE: A mink stole.

BEN: A mink stole, yes, thank you. A mink stole draped around her neck. I walk towards her. She looks up at me. She throws her arms out and pulls me down beside her. She holds onto me or I hold onto her, I'm not sure which. She's singing. And the song –
There's something –

A boy appears.

Everything around me becomes dark. My head starts to ache. A sharp pain behind my eyes and in my mouth.

The sound of the violin becomes louder and discordant.

I put my hands on the old woman's face to quiet her. I press them firmly against her mouth and her nose. She stops moving.
I take the mink stole off her body and clutch onto it. I feel heavy. Everything feels heavy.
The old woman becomes stiff. A strange odour comes off her. I start to feel sick.
I grab her arms. I drag her down the corridor. I throw her body down one of the metal incinerating shafts.
I go back to my room. I sit down on my inflatable mattress and I write a beautiful, stirring melody for the children.

SCENE EIGHTEEN

MYA: I get up in the middle of the night. I go up to one of the Security men.
'Let's go out on the ice. You and me. Take me for a midnight ride.' We sneak into one of the vehicles. We drive around the ice.
'Take me back to the old Complex. I left something there. Something valuable. I need to find it.'

I put my hand on his leg. He parks the vehicle. He unlocks a door. I tell him to wait. He tells me to be careful. I pull my sweater over my head and run through the corridors. The Woodpecker Wing. Leroy's room. He's not there. His bed is empty. Some men are sprawled out on the floor. They see me staring at Leroy's bed.

'The Dutch kid. He fell off the scaffolding. Head first onto the ice. They threw his body down one of the incinerators.'

I fumble around. I crawl into Leroy's bed. Something hard under my back. A small leather notebook. The writing is scratchy and uneven. It's all in Dutch. I don't understand it but I read it anyway.

Mya reads the following lines in Dutch, Leroy reads them in English.

I was named after the song 'Bad Bad Leroy Brown.'
Ik was genoemd naar he lied 'Bad Bad Leroy Brown.'

I had asthma when I was a child and slept in a plastic tent.
Ik has asthma toen ik kind was en in een plactic tent sliep.

I sat on bridges and threw rocks at boats.
Ik zat op bruggen en goodie stenen naar boten.

I ate ice cream and chased squirrels.
Ik at ijs en joeg eekhhoorntjes na.

I put leaves in books.
ik legde bladeren in boeken.

There was a vacation on a boat.
Er was een vacantie op een boot.

A camp near a lake.
Een kamp bij een meer.

A lamb dinner.
Een maaltijd met lamsvlees.

A Norwegian singer.
Een Norse zanger.

A Russian prostitute.
Een Russische prostituee.

A sister.
Eeen zusje.

A paper hat.
Een papieren hoed.

Or was it –

MYA: Some kind of diary, I guess. A ... what do you call it? A testimonial. A manifesto.

Everything was a conspiracy to Leroy. Everything was a lie. 'You can't know anyone,' Leroy used to say. 'You go to bed. You shut your eyes. You're alone. Everything's gone. Nothing's there.'

A white cloth is lying on the floor beside his bed. On the material, his skin, his hair, his sweat, his face.

I leave the notebook on the bed. I put the white cloth in my pocket.

The Security man drives me back across the ice. He comes into my room. I take the white cloth out of my pocket. I tell the Security man to put it over his face. He winks at me. He grabs the back of my neck.

SCENE NINETEEN

CLARE: It literally takes the breath out of your body. Looking at it all lit up. A sprawling network of buildings with various levels, enclosed walkways, vaulted roofs, metallic panels. Everything large and glowing. A long red carpet outside the main entrance lined with ice sculptures and coloured lights.

People are arriving by boat. There's going to be dancing,

music, fireworks, fresh oysters, barbecued salmon, champagne, a parade with masks and kites, children dressed up as dogs, pulling sleds.

It's amazing, the things people are capable of.

All the Residents have been given small gifts of appreciation for all their hard work: sweet little cupcakes.

ASH: They take my penguin figurines away. They're giving them to visiting dignitaries as gifts and they're going to sell the rest in the Centre's new gift shop.

They ask me to come with them to the new Complex. They say it will be better there.

I could make more penguins, they say. Maybe some whales, some seals, maybe some giant squids because giant squids might be fun.

They say this is my last chance. I shut my eyes. The door closes.

A cupcake with a small blue insignia appears.

ASH: In the centre of the room, there's a cupcake. The cupcake has blue icing and a tiny sugar candy in the middle of it – a fish or a dolphin or something. The moon shines on it through the window. Everything else around me is dark.

I pick up the cupcake. I go downstairs. I wander through the corridors.

There's still many of us left here. People who chose to stay or were too sick to be moved. They've left the ventilation on. We can't turn it off. Bodies are piled up in the corridors. People are wheezing, stumbling around.

Everything is lost.

I stuff the cupcake into my mouth. The icing is thick and heavy. The sugar candy gets stuck in my throat.

I can't –

I slide down the wall onto the floor.

SCENE TWENTY

CLARE: Ben.

BEN: Clare.

CLARE: You must be all revved up.

BEN: Well, the children are excited.

CLARE: It's a big night.

BEN: They've all had baths and haircuts and they've given us new ties to wear, so –

CLARE: I think you're all going to look sharp, you're all going to do fine.

BEN: There are some men coming to record the concert, so there's a lot of pressure, knowing it will be preserved forever.

CLARE: Yes, or for a long time at least.

BEN: There's also been some talk about setting up some kind of tour, if things go well, to other Recovery Centres. Central Australia, Dubai, the Orkney Islands, Utah –

CLARE: Utah. Well, that's something.

Alex enters with a violin.

ALEX: Ben?

BEN: Hello.

ALEX: One of the strings popped.

BEN: That's not good.

ALEX: I was just bowing it, and –

BEN: I'll see what I can do.

ALEX: Okey-dokey.

Ben leaves with the violin.

CLARE: Sorry, I don't think I've seen you before. What's your name?

ALEX: Alex.

CLARE: Alex. Alexander. Alexander the Great.

ALEX: Well, Alex.

CLARE: And so you –
You're –
You play the –

ALEX: The violin.

CLARE: The –
I'm sorry –

THE END

ACKNOWLEDGEMENTS

Influences, inspiration and thanks: Brightblack Morning Light, Sigur Rós, Sionnach and Saoirse, the Brothers Grimm, Wallace Shawn, the Lesbian Cottage on rue Drolet, Vanessa Porteous, Lise Ann Johnson, Craig Hall, Stacey Christodoulous, Playwrights' Workshop Montreal, the Antarctic Treaty of 1955, Werner Herzog, *Selling Sickness: How the World's Biggest Pharmaceutical Companies Are Turning Us All into Patients*, Tulum, Mexico, Taboo, the Carter family (not Nick and Aaron – the one with Maybelle, A. P. and Sara), Godspeed You! Black Emperor, Famke, the Okanagan Valley, graffiti, my family.

ABOUT THE AUTHOR

Greg MacArthur is a playwright and actor. His plays have been produced across Canada, as well as in South Africa, Germany and the UK. His writing credits include: *Recovery*, *Get Away*, *Snowman*, *girls! girls! girls!*, *Epiphany*, *The Rise and Fall of Peter Gaveston* and *Beggar Boy* (a play for children). He was the co-founder and co−artistic director of House of Slacks, a collaborative theatre company based in Toronto whose work included *The Millennium Project* and *Stem*. His plays have been translated into German and French. He is currently Artist-in-Residence at Playwrights' Workshop Montreal.

Typeset in Sabon Next and Copperplate
Printed and bound at the Coach House on bpNichol Lane, 2007

Edited and designed by Christina Palassio
Cover image by Jordan Bent (*Lost Child*, Acrylic on Hot Press
Watercolor Stock, 6 x 9 inches)
www.jordanbent.com

Coach House Books
401 Huron Street (rear) on bpNichol Lane
Toronto, Ontario
M5S 2G5

416 979 2217
800 367 6360

mail@chbooks.com
www.chbooks.com